Henry Ward Beecher

Aids to prayer

Henry Ward Beecher

Aids to prayer

ISBN/EAN: 9783337284022

Printed in Europe, USA, Canada, Australia, Japan

Cover: Foto ©Lupo / pixelio.de

More available books at **www.hansebooks.com**

AIDS TO PRAYER.

BY

HENRY WARD BEECHER.

"More things are wrought by prayer
Than this world dreams of. . . . . . .
  For what are men better than sheep or goats,
That nourish a blind life within the brain,
If, knowing God, they lift not hands of prayer
Both for themselves and those who call them friend?
For so the whole round earth is every way
Bound by gold chains about the feet of God."

TENNYSON.

NEW-YORK:
ANSON D. F. RANDOLPH, 770 BROADWAY,
CORNER OF NINTH STREET.

1866.

The contents of this book do not appear in type for the first time. Many of the things were originally published in THE INDEPENDENT, *or in sermons, or in the* LIFE THOUGHTS. *The reader may be curious to know why they should be again published in America. There is a history in the fact. Mr. Randolph received a copy of this book from England, where it had been compiled and published without giving credit to the Author: supposing it to be an English production, the American Publisher put it into print, and only then was led to suspect it was a compilation from my writings.*

If this very comely little volume shall carry the truth to any who would have missed it but for this English appropriation, we shall esteem it a happy end to a transaction not altogether ingenuous on the part of the English publisher.

H. W. BEECHER.

CONTENTS.

	PAGE
INTRODUCTION,	5
OUR FATHER,	15
GOD'S TENDER MERCY,	33
THE REASON OF PRAYER,	51
THE GREAT EXEMPLAR,	77
"COME BOLDLY TO THE THRONE,"	91
THE SCOPE OF PRAYER,	113
THE AID OF THE SPIRIT,	125
HUMILITY BEFORE GOD,	139
THE PRAYER-MEETING,	147
THE PRAYERLESS LIFE,	159
APPENDIX,	171

Introduction.

Acts xvii. 25–28.

"He giveth to all life, and breath, and all things; and hath made of one blood all nations of men for to dwell on all the face of the earth; and hath determined the times before appointed, and the bounds of their habitation; that they should seek the Lord, if haply they might feel after him, and find him, though he be not far from every one of us: for in him we live, and move, and have our being; as certain also of your own poets have said, For we are also his offspring."

1 Thess. v. 17.
"Pray without ceasing."

1 Tim. ii. 8.
"I will therefore that men pray every where, lifting up holy hands, without wrath and doubting."

Isa. lv. 6–7.
"Seek ye the Lord while he may be found, call ye upon him while he is near. Let the wicked forsake his way, and the unrighteous man his thoughts: and let him return unto the Lord, and he will have mercy upon him: and to our God, for he will abundantly pardon."

Ps. xxxiv. 10.
"The young lions do lack, and suffer hunger: but they that seek the Lord shall not want any good thing."

"My God! is any hour so sweet,
   From blush of morn to evening star,
As that which calls me to Thy feet,
      The hour of prayer?

"Blest is the tranquil hour of morn,
   And blest that hour of solemn eve,
When, on the wings of prayer upborne,
      The world I leave.

"Then is my strength by Thee renewed;
   Then are my sins by Thee forgiven;
Then dost thou cheer my solitude
      With hopes of heaven.

"No words can tell what sweet relief
   There for my every want I find;
What strength for warfare, balm for grief,
      What peace of mind.

"Hushed is each doubt, gone every fear
   My spirit seems in heaven to stay;
And e'en the penitential tear
      Is wiped away.

"Lord! till I reach that blissful shore
   No privilege so dear shall be,
As thus my inmost soul to pour
      In prayer to Thee."

                CHARLOTTE ELLIOTT.

Introduction.

WE have always been affected by the petition of the disciples to the Saviour, "Lord, teach us how to pray." How many yet would fain address the same request, with simplicity and conscious want, to Christ!

If the first moments of the morning, the very first thoughts of the day are given to prayer, it will be found, at least in many cases, to give direction to the feelings of the whole day. The keynote of the day is struck early. And, simple as it may seem, we have forced a few moments in the morning to hold the day to its course, as a rudder does the ship. Some persons, we suspect, fail of interest in prayer by attempting to pray by the clock. They have been taught that a regular time and an appointed place are eminently beneficial. They have tried the time with so many failures, that the place, by association and memory of ill success, becomes disgustful. We are not about to say that punctuality and regularity are not good, but only that they are not alike good for all; and that when experience shows that they hinder and do not help, Christians are under no law to the clock. Persons of regulated feelings, of methodical habits, and of uniform occupations, find great advantage in stated hours of prayer. People of mercurial dispositions, who live without special arrangement and system, will find, on the contrary, that such attempts at punctuality will not help them, except as an exercise in method and regularity.

If a man should insist upon wallowing in the sand when the tide was out, because he had made up his mind to bathe in one place and at one hour, he would not be much unlike him who prays when his watch, and not when his heart, tells him the time. Christians are to remember that they are children of liberty. They are not bound up, as the Jews were, to times and seasons, to places and methods. Prayer may become a yoke of superstition, instead of the wings of liberty.

It may be briefly said, take notice of the times when prayer is refreshing. Learn from your own experience how and when prayer is best for you. You are under bonds to no man, be he minister or layman.

We think that one may very much aid himself, by taking a few moments of his brightest hours for silent prayer. The Jews were taught to present their best fruits for offerings. We should not choose refuse hours, good for nothing else, to pray in. No matter where you are, nor what you are doing, send a glance Godward from the top of every exalted hour — as from a hill-top, a child, going home, would strive to catch a glimpse of his father's house. In this manner, after a little, the soul would lay up remembrances of many sweet and noble experiences, and would fight discouragements by hope drawn from past success.

We suspect that many persons mar this enjoyment by very erroneous ideas of quantity. They read of eminent Christians who pray by the hour, they hear sermons upon the wrestling of Jacob with the angel, and, above all, they are told that Christ prayed all night. They, therefore, attempt immense prayer. Of course, they fail. A man might as well attempt to imitate the old prophets who ate in preparation of forty days' fast. If a man is moved to pray only five minutes, it is his duty to stop there. If he is moved to pray an hour, he is at liberty to do so. But in every case prayer is to be regulated by your own inward want, and not from the outside by somebody's example. Indeed, we meet every day with persons who would be injured by long praying. They have but little to say. If Christ were on earth, and they were disciples, they would listen rather than speak. There is communion by thinking as well as speaking. There is unuttered prayer as well as vocal. Thoughts that roll silently are more significant, often, than those which can clothe themselves in words. It is possible to pray too much. That is always too much which is beyond your real want or desire.

Christians bring themselves into trouble by very false ideas of prayer. They select impassioned prayers as models, and judge themselves to be praying in proportion as they approach these examples. But what if your wants are few, your feelings tranquil, your thoughts simple, and your whole mind and experience formed upon a different basis? Is prayer some objective exercise to be copied?

or is it the presenting before God of just what you think, feel, or need?

One single sentence is a sufficient prayer. There is no one who can not command his thoughts long enough for that. If your thoughts wander, the probability is that you are trying to pray too much. Be shorter. Say just as much as there is in you to say. If there is nothing, say nothing; if little, say little; silence is better than mockery. Consider the Lord's Prayer — how short, how simple! It contains the whole world's want, and yet a little child can use it.

Accept prayer as liberty, and not a bondage. Use it in any manner that will be of profit. Go often and tarry but a little, or go and tarry all night, if you will, upon the mount. You pray, if there is but one sentence — God be merciful to me a sinner — just as freely as if there were a thousand besides.

"Lord, what a change within us one short hour
Spent in Thy presence will prevail to make,
What heavy burdens from our bosoms take,
What parched grounds refresh, as with a shower!
We kneel, and all around us seems to lower;
We rise, and all the distant and the near,
Stands forth in sunny outline, brave and clear;
We kneel, how weak!—we rise, how full of power!
Why, therefore, should we do ourselves this wrong,
Or others—that we are not always strong,
That we are ever overborne with care,
That we should ever weak or heartless be,
Anxious or troubled, when with us is prayer,
And joy, and strength, and courage are with Thee?"
THE DEAN OF WESTMINSTER.

"What wondrous grace! who knows its full extent?
A creature, dust and ashes, speaks with God—
Tells all his woes—enumerates his wants—
Yea, pleads with Deity, and gains relief.
'Tis prayer, yes, 'tis 'effectual, fervent prayer,'
Puts dignity on worms—proves life divine—
Makes demons tremble—breaks the darkest cloud,
And with a princely power prevails with God!
And shall this privilege become a task?
My God, forbid! pour out Thy Spirit's grace,
Draw me by love, and teach me how to pray.
Yea, let Thy holy unction from above,
Beget, extend, maintain my intercourse,
With Father, Son, and Spirit, Israel's God,
Until petitions are exchanged for praise."
IRONS.

Our Father.

GAL. iv. 6.

"And because ye are sons, God hath sent forth the Spirit of his Son into your hearts, crying, Abba, Father."

MATT. vi. 6–13.

"When thou prayest, enter into thy closet; and when thou hast shut thy door, pray to thy Father which is in secret; and thy Father, which seeth in secret, shall reward thee openly. But when ye pray, use not vain repetitions, as the heathen do: for they think that they shall be heard for their much speaking. Be not ye therefore like unto them: for your Father knoweth what things ye have need of before ye ask him. After this manner therefore pray ye:

Our Father, which art in heaven,
Hallowed be thy name.
Thy kingdom come.
Thy will be done in earth as it is in heaven.
Give us this day our daily bread.
And forgive us our debts, as we forgive our debtors.
And lead us not into temptation; but deliver us from evil:
For thine is the kingdom, and the power, and the glory,
Forever. Amen."

Ps. ciii. 13.

"Like as a father pitieth his children, so the Lord pitieth them that fear him."

"Our God, our Father, with us stay,
And make us keep Thy narrow way;
Free us from sin and all its power;
Give us a joyful dying hour;
Deliver us from Satan's arts,
And let us build our hopes on Thee,
Down in our very heart of hearts!
O God! may we true servants be,
And serve Thee ever perfectly.
Help us, with all Thy children here,
To fight and flee with holy fear;
Flee from temptation, and to fight
With Thine own weapons for the right;
Amen, Amen, so let it be!
So shall we ever sing to Thee,
         Hallelujah!"

                        MARTIN LUTHER.

"Now thank we all our God,
   With heart and hands and voices,
Who wondrous things hath done,
   In whom His world rejoices;
Who from our mother's arms
   Hath blessed us on our way
With countless gifts of love,
   And still is ours to-day.

"Oh may this bounteous God
   Through all our life be near us,
With ever-joyful hearts
   And blessed peace to cheer us;
And keep us in His grace,
   And guide us when perplexed,
And free us from all ills
   In this world and the next.

"All praise and thanks to God
   The Father now be given,
The Son, and Him who reigns
   With them in highest heaven;
The one Eternal God,
   Whom earth and heaven adore;
For thus it was, is now,
   And shall be evermore!"

"Our Father."

IN a true Christian's devout aspirations, it is not from instruction or habit, but from spontaneous impulse, that he exclaims, "Our Father!" His thoughts go out after God. His heart yearns for Him. His soul longs, with unutterable longings, for His abiding presence. He comes with a truly filial spirit before God, and it is perfectly easy and natural for him to say, "Our Father." And he has a right to say it. He is the child of God, and he knows it; for "the Spirit itself beareth witness with our spirits that we are the children of God." Being the child of his Father, and away from his Father's house, he yearns for it, and at times is homesick—as children that are kept at school away from their parents long for the day of vacation, that they may go home; and these yearnings are the testimony of the Spirit that we are the children of God. The man who has these feelings, and has them habitually, need not hesitate to call himself a child of God, or to address God as "Our Father."

There are some Christians who always seem to have entire and unwavering faith in God as their Father. They trust in Him to such a degree as to believe that whatever may be the happenings of Providence, everything will be for the best, and that they will be taken care of, and never left alone. They are confident in Him, and seem never for a moment to doubt. Their cup always runs over, because they always think it runs over. But, on the other hand, there are others who, while they are blessed abundantly, never see or think that they are blessed at all. And this class comprises the multitude of men. They call God "Our Father," only because the Lord's Prayer begins so, and not because their own prayer naturally and spontaneously confesses that they are His children, and that He is their Father. They have doubts and glooms. They have fightings without, and fears within. They allow small things to perplex them, and great things to overwhelm them. They distrust God — not intentionally, but really. They doubt His providence, though they would hardly believe that they doubt. They habitually look on the dark side of things, and excuse themselves for it by saying that they are constitutionally melancholy; whereas the fault is nothing more nor less than a practical want of faith. It is an unconscious scepticism of God. Men theoretically extol their faith, but practically deny it. They give way before every trouble, instead of conquering it; and in every dark hour flee for refuge, not to God, but to themselves.

Now, all Christians, whether hopeful or despondent, are sometimes like the disciples on the Sea of Galilee — driven hither and thither by contrary winds. They toil all the night upon the deep, casting their nets, but taking nothing. Nay, oftentimes, their sea is without a Christ walking upon the water, and their ship without a Christ even asleep. Yet when they desire His coming upon the sea, and cry out to Him, they soon see Him walking to them over the waves. When they desire His awakening in the ship, they soon see Him rising to rebuke the wind, saying, "Peace, be still," until there is a great calm. God hides his face only to disclose it again; and His hidings are oftentimes as full of mercy as His manifested presence. But whether to their feeble-sighted eyes He is present or absent, they may always know that "He is not far from them at any time." When there are clouds so that they can not see Him, they may look at Him through faith, and discern that He is not far off. And as they that go down upon the deep, and are overmastered by storms in the darkness of the night, knowing not on what strange shores they may be thrown, cast anchor and wait for day, so in the midst of trial and temptation, when the storm is fierce and the night is dark, when the lights are quenched and the signals gone, they may at least cast anchor; and if they wait in faith and hope for the day, it will surely dawn. The darkness will always hide itself, and the light appear. There never was a night so long that the day did not overtake it. There never was a morning without its morning star. There never was a day without its sun.

God can reveal himself to His own people as He does not to the world. He can give to every Christian heart, to the timid as well as to the strong, to the sorrowing as well as to the hopeful, those divine intimations, those precious thoughts, those sweet-breathed feelings, which are evidence that His Spirit dwelleth in them. He can inspire the heart with that perfect love which casteth out fear. He can take away all doubts and misgivings, all gloomy misapprehensions, all dreary forebodings of the future. He can make sunshine out of shadow, and day out of midnight. When our fears have been like growing thorns in our side, He can pluck away the thorns, and heal the wounds; and He can turn every spear which has pierced us into a rod and staff, which, instead of wounding, shall support us; so that the very things which once cast us down may be made to hold us up. He can so deal with us as to make every yoke easy and every burden light; so that the heavy laden may come to Him to be relieved of their loads. He can touch the fountains of our sorrow, and make our tears like gems and crystals, more precious than pearls or diamonds. Our tears are oftentimes among His most precious treasures. The things that we call treasures He counts as of very little worth. The human soul is His treasury, out of which He coins unspeakable riches. Thoughts and feelings, desires and yearnings, faith and hope—these are the most precious things which God finds in us.

He can do all things for us, whatsoever we need, and more than we need. We are too slow to believe in His generosity. We do not often enough think that as He has infinite desires to help us, so also He has infinite powers. He is able to carry out all that He can ever wish for us. God is not like man. Our means are limited. With us, wishing to possess is far from possessing; wishing to do is far from doing; but with Him, the wish and the power are one. His desires are fully equalled by His means. He is "able to do exceeding abundantly above all that we can ask or think." Things that are great to us are small to Him. The favours that we ask of Him seem to us to be large and royal; yet to Him they are very little things. The gifts He has power to bestow are not only greater than we ever ask, but ever can ask, or even think.

He is always willing to give special grace for special emergency. If men are suddenly brought into trouble, He is " a very present help in time of need." When rich men, by some unexpected reverse of fortune, are made poor, He can sustain them under their burdens, when without Him they would be utterly crushed. When friends are parted from friends, when families are broken and scattered by death, when the mother loses her child, and weeps because the cradle is no longer to be rocked, and the sweet laugh is hushed in the house, God can give "the oil of joy for mourning." Whenever His children suffer disappointment, when clouds cast shadows over their path, when troubles brood heavily before them, when they are in trials of business or in greater trials of bereavement, He can take off the heavy weights. He can make the rough places smooth, and the crooked ways straight. When sorrow comes that seems to forbid all consolation, He can gently wipe away the tears, and bring back joy and hope once more.

He is a physician who only waits to be called; He is a friend who longs to be trusted; He is a helper who only wants us to ask His aid. But He wants us to ask Him heartily and truthfully. He wishes us to reach up our hand, and take covenant by His hand. He desires us to cast our care upon Him, for He careth for us. He commands us to confide entirely in Him. He wants us to have no hesitancy in our faith.

And this is reasonable. It is what men ask every day of their own children. A father expects his child to confide in him. A child expects to trust freely in his father. And we ought to go to God, being His children. with less distrust and more confidence. We ought to take Him at His word, and to have faith in His promises. If He has said, "I will never leave thee nor forsake thee," we ought boldly to say, "The Lord is my helper; I will not fear what man shall do unto me."

But when we borrow trouble, and look forward into the future to see what storms are coming, and distress ourselves before they come as to how we shall avert them if they ever do come, we lose our proper trustfulness in God. When we torment ourselves with imaginary dangers, or trials, or reverses, we have already parted with that perfect love which casteth out fear. Mothers sometimes fret themselves, and are made miserable about the future career of their children — whether they will turn out drunkards or not, whether they will go to the gallows or not, whether they will be a disgrace to their parentage or not. Now, all this is simply an evidence of a lack of faith. There are many persons in good health, with all their faculties in active exercise, who, having nothing else to worry about, rob themselves of sleep at night by thinking, "if they should suddenly be taken away, what would become of their families, and who would take care of their children?" Such distrust of God is dishonourable to Christian men; and it is only because of His exceeding patience — which is the most wonderful attribute of the Divine nature — that He does not signally rebuke and punish it whenever it is manifested. When persons are taken sick, they ought to bear it with a good grace; but nine out of ten, even among Christian men, repine and murmur.

When they are visited with any trouble, their first thought is apt to be, "How grievously I am afflicted!" though the nobler thought would be, "How graciously I am sustained!" When a cross is laid upon them, they cry out, "What a burden I have to carry!" whereas they might better say, "What a burden Christ carries for me!" A Christian sailor, who lost one of his legs in the battle of Trafalgar, said that he could very often measure the faith of the people who conversed with him by the way in which they alluded to his misfortune. Nine out of every ten would exclaim, "What a pity that you lost your leg?" and only one in ten, "What a blessing that the other was preserved!" When God comes into the family and takes away one child, instead of complaining because He has taken one, it would be wiser to thank Him that He has left the rest. Or He may crush a man's business, and strip him of all his worldly wealth, and yet leave untouched and uninvaded what is dearer than all—the cradle of his only child. Would it not be nobler for such a man to be thankful for what God left than to murmur for what He took away? "The Lord giveth, and the Lord taketh away," but He always gives more than He takes away. If God robs a man of his riches, He leaves him his health, which is better than riches. If He takes health, He leaves wealth. If He takes both, He leaves friends. And if He takes all these—house, and home, and worldly goods—God's providence is not yet exhausted, and He can make blessings out of other things which remain. He never strips a man entirely bare. A man may be left a beggar upon the highway, and yet be able to give unceasing testimony to God's goodness and grace.

If men were to give thanks to God for what He permits them to have, rather than to utter complaints for what He wisely and graciously withholds, He might not unlikely give to them more abundantly, if for no other reason than to increase their gratitude. An old man, who is now without home or friends, a stranger in a strange land, who earns a scanty crust of bread, day by day, by selling steel-pens and writing-paper from street to street, said the other day, that though he had several times been so reduced as to be for a period of forty-eight hours and longer without a morsel to eat, he never lost his trust in Providence, and always rebuked himself whenever he complained at his lot! This man's faith was genuine! He was a hero in rags, greater than many a hero in armour!

God's goodness is large and generous; only our faith in it is small and mean. He carries the whole globe in His thoughtful providence, easier than a mother carries a babe in her arms. If we cannot see the end from the beginning, what matters it so long as He sees it? What have we to do but to seek first the kingdom of God and His righteousness, and leave the rest in faith to Him?

We ought not to forget that an affectionate, confiding, tender faith, habitually exercised, would save us half the annoyances of life, for it would lift us up above the reach of them. If an eagle were to fly low along the ground, every man might aim a dart at it, but when it soars into the clouds, it is above every arrow's reach. And they that trust in God "shall mount up with wings as eagles; they shall run and not be weary; and they shall walk and not faint." Christ's invitation is—" Come unto me, all ye that labour and are heavy laden, and I will give you rest. Take my yoke upon you, and learn of me; for I am meek and lowly in heart; and ye shall find rest unto your soul. For my yoke is easy, and my burden is light."

God's Tender Mercy.

Ps. ciii. 8–10.

"The Lord is merciful and gracious, slow to anger, and plenteous in mercy. He will not always chide; neither will he keep his anger for ever. He hath not dealt with us after our sins, nor rewarded us according to our iniquities."

Ps. xxxvi. 7–9.

"How excellent is thy loving-kindness, O God! therefore the children of men put their trust under the shadow of thy wings. They shall be abundantly satisfied with the fatness of thy house; and thou shalt make them drink of the river of thy pleasures. For with thee is the fountain of life: in thy light shall we see light."

Ps. xxiii.

"The Lord is my shepherd, I shall not want. He maketh me to lie down in green pastures: he leadeth me beside the still waters. He restoreth my soul: he leadeth me in the paths of righteousness for his name's sake. Yea, though I walk through the valley of the shadow of death, I will fear no evil: for thou art with me; thy rod and thy staff they comfort me. Thou preparest a table before me in the presence of mine enemies: thou anointest my head with oil; my cup runneth over. Surely goodness and mercy shall follow me all the days of my life; and I will dwell in the house of the Lord for ever."

Ps. lxxxvi. 5, 6.

"For thou, Lord, art good, and ready to forgive; and plenteous in mercy unto all them that call upon thee. Give ear, O Lord, unto my prayer; and attend to the voice of my supplications."

Micah vii. 18, 19.

"Who is a God like unto thee, that pardoneth iniquity, and passeth by the transgression of the remnant of his heritage? he retaineth not his anger for ever, because he delighteth in mercy. He will turn again, he will have compassion upon us; he will subdue our iniquities: and thou wilt cast all their sins into the depths of the sea."

"What a gracious God have we!
In His gifts of grace how free!
How intent our prayers to hear,
And to them that pray how near!
How to balmy mercy prone,
And to kind compassion!
How regardfully He wakes
For His chosen servants' sakes!
How He gives them grace to pray,
And then to their suits give way!
How He prompts each good desire,
And blows up that spark to fire.
He hath set no greater task
To obtain of Him but 'Ask.'
No exacter search to find,
But to seek with humble mind;
No more pains heaven to unlock,
But with spotless hand to knock—
Yet he joys to see man press Him,
And to wrestle till He bless him."

"Preserve, O Lord! within our hearts
  The memory of Thy favour,
That else insensibly departs,
  And loses its sweet savour!
Lodge it within us! As the power of light
Lives inexhaustibly in precious gems
Fixed on the front of eastern diadems,
So shine our thankfulness for ever bright."

WORDSWORTH.

God's Tender Mercy.

HOW strange it seems to fall upon those wonderful lyrics in the psalms of David, singing to us out of the rude ages of the past, where we naturally expect harshness and severity! How wonderful that our age should go back to this old warrior to learn tenderness!—that the most exquisite views of Divine compassion should spring forth from the world's untrained periods, from Moses, the shepherd and legislator of the desert, and from David, the sweet singer of Israel, whose hand was mightiest among the mighty, whether laid upon the strings of the bow or of the harp!

Noble old warrior! Thou didst send dismay to thine enemies, and breathe joy among thy friends. Thy bow abode in strength, and thine arrows were terrible in the day of battle. But those silver shafts of song, from a lyre surpassing the fabled sweetness of Apollo's, have sped through the dusky years, through thousands of them, and are flying yet; not for wounding, but for life and healing.

If we remember the times of David, we shall be no less surprised at the ripeness of the views of God which he gives, their symmetry and all-sidedness, gentle without moral weakness, and strong without harshness; building up the Divine glory in justice and truth, and walling it about with majesty and stability. But then, as in a garden enclosed with mighty walls, O Psalmist, thou didst cover the bosom of God with flowers and fruits, and make the thought of Him sweeter to the fainting soul than all the breath of flowers or sound of cooling waters!

As but a few years intervened between the era of David and of Homer—not the measure of a man's lifetime—it is interesting to observe the views which they held, synchronously, of the character of God. While David was filling Jerusalem with these matchless lyrics, Homer, the blind wanderer of Greece, whom the world has since made a universal citizen, was singing of the Grecian gods. If any one would know the glory of the Hebrew bard, let him contrast the Psalms of David with Homeric representations of God. How could Greece be so dark when such a star shone over Mount Zion? How could Olympus be so mean while Sinai flamed with such grandeur? Living in the same day, a thousand years of religion divided them. Our hearts decide in a moment which was the true prophet, and the teacher of the true God.

Let us select from David's chants but the single strain—*God's Tender Mercy.*

Pity is a mode or particular development of benevolence. It is sympathy for persons on account of weakness or suffering. It is not mere compassion, but is mingled with a desire to aid and relieve. Pity and compassion are the antitheses of those affections by which we take hold of men who are good, lovely, desirable for their grace of nobleness and purity; or of those who are prosperous, strong, and happy. For such, to be sure, we have a lively sympathy, but it is of a different sort. God has gladness for those who are glad, and pity for those who are sad.

The pity of God, as disclosed in this psalm, is the working out of the whole Divine nature of goodness toward the human family, in their unformed, immature, sinful, struggling existence. The race was not born perfect — men were sown as seeds are. They come of germs, turn to leaves, shoot forth a slender stem, grow little by little to branches, and find firmness and solidity only after a long probation of weakness, temptation, sin, and all its sorrows. This is true of individual men. It is true historically of mankind. The need of compassion for the race has been just as great as is the need in every household of compassion towards babes and young children. It is still the need of each man and of the whole world.

As much crime as there is, calling for punishment—as much deliberate wrong, to be met by deliberate justice—as much licence as there is, and overflowing passion and desolating lust—there is even more ignorance, mistake, sorrowful weakness, and unwitting evil. The world wanders like a half-grown orphan, calling for aid without answer, and weeps for trouble, and wanders still, stumbling through ages. And though it needs reproof and correction, it needs kindness more. Though it needs the grasp of the strong hand, it needs, too, the open palm of love and tenderness. It requires punishment; but it needs pity even more than avenging justice.

While, therefore, the Divine character

drawn in the Bible hath great depth of shadow in justice, all its salient points stand forth in the high lights of love and mercy! God is full of near, real, overflowing, and inexhaustible compassion for man!

But it is declared that God's pity is not simply pity—*it is a father's pity.*

If a man be found weltering by the road, wounded, and a stranger comes who never before had even seen him, he will pity him. No matter if born under a different heaven, or speaking a different tongue, or worshipping at a different altar, he pities him; for the heart of man speaks one language the world over, and suffering wakes compassion.

But if, instead of being a stranger, it were a near neighbour, how much more and more tender the pity, as he ran to his help! But if, instead of one who stood only in the offices of general and neighbourhood kindness, it were a strong personal friend — yea, a brother — how much more intense would be the throbbing emotion of tenderness and pity!

But all these fade away before the wild outcry of the man's own father, who would give his life for his son, and who gives pity, now, not by measure, but with such a volume that it is as if a soul were gushing out in all its life!

But the noblest heart on earth is but a trickling stream from a faint and wasting fountain, compared with the ineffable soul and heart of God, the everlasting Father! The pity of God is like a father's, in all that is tender, strong, and full, but not in scope and power. For every one of God's feelings moves in the sphere of the infinite. His pity has all the scope and divinity which belong to power, wisdom, justice! Yea, power, wisdom, and justice are God's lesser ways, and come towards that side of His being where there would be restriction, if anywhere; while love and mercy are God's peculiar glory. In these He finds the most glorious liberty of the Divine nature.

Nothing so soon wears out and exhausts men as deep feelings and strong sympathies, especially those which have in them an element of pain, as pity hath. Our life requires to be broken in two each day, and replanted, that it may spring up again from sleep, as new blossoms out of soil. We are buried every night for a resurrection of each morning; and thus our life is not a continuous line, unbroken, but a series of lives and deaths, of deaths and births.

But God, in His almightiness, asks no rest and requires no slumber, but holds straight on without weariness, wearing out the ages, Himself unworn; changing all things, Himself without variableness or shadow of turning! God is like the sun at noon, that casts down straight rays, and so throws down the shadows upon the ground underneath each tree; but He never, like the sun, goes westward towards his setting, turning all shadows from under the trees, and slanting them upon the ground. God stands in eternal fulness, like a sun that knows neither morning, nor evening, nor night, but only noon, and noon always!

God's pity abides, even as He abides, and partakes of the Divine grandeur and omnipotence. There is a whole eternity in it for substance and duration. As God himself cannot be measured with lines of latitude and longitude, but is boundless, so is His every attribute. His pity is infinite, moving with equal step to all the other attributes of God, and holding its course and path as far forth as omniscience doth; it paces with omnipresence along the circuits of infinity! For as heaven is high above the earth, so great is His mercy towards them that fear Him. As far as the east is from the west, so far hath He removed our transgressions from us!

God's pity is not as some sweet cordial,

poured in dainty drops from a golden phial. It is not like the musical water-drops of some slender rill, murmuring down the dark sides of Mount Sinai. It is wide as the whole cope of heaven. It is abundant as all the air. If one had art to gather up all the golden sunlight that to-day falls wide over all this continent—falling through every silent hour; and all that is dispersed over the whole ocean, flashing from every wave; and all that is poured refulgent over the northern wastes of ice, and along the whole continent of Europe, and the vast outlying Asia, and torrid Africa; if one could in anywise gather up this immense and incalculable outflow and treasure of sunlight that falls down through the bright hours, and runs in liquid ether about the mountains, and fills all the plains, and sends innumerable rays through every secret place, pouring over and filling every flower, shining down the sides of every blade of grass, resting in glorious humility upon the humblest things—on stick, and stone, and pebble; on the spider's web, the sparrow's nest, the threshold of the young foxes' hole, where they play and warm themselves; —that rests on the prisoner's window, that strikes radiant beams through the slave's tear, that puts gold upon the widow's weeds, that plates and roofs the city with burnished gold, and goes on in its wild abundance up and down the earth, shining everywhere and always, since the day of primal creation, without faltering, without stint, without waste or diminution; as full, as fresh, as overflowing to-day as if it were the very first day of its outplay — if one might gather up this boundless, endless, infinite treasure, to measure it, then might he tell the height and depth, and unending glory of the pity of God! The light, and the sun its source, are God's own figures of the immensity and copiousness of His mercy and compassion (Ps. lxxxiv. 11, 12; Isa. lv. 6–13.)

This Divine pity applies to us on account of our weakness. God looks upon our littleness, as compared with His angels that excel in strength, much, it may be supposed, as we look upon little children as compared with grown-up men.

Divine pity is also exercised in view of our sufferings, both of body and of mind. We sometimes fear to bring our troubles to God, because they must seem so small to Him who sitteth on the circle of the earth. But if they are large enough to vex and endanger our welfare, they are large enough to touch His heart of love. For love does not measure by a merchant's scales, nor with a surveyor's chain. It hath a delicacy which is unknown in any handling of material substances.

It sometimes seems as if God cared for nothing. The wicked are at ease. The good are vexed incessantly. The world is full of misrule and confusion. The darling of the flock is always made the sacrifice. Some child in the very midst of its glee becomes suddenly silent—as a music-box, its spring giving way, stops in the midst of its strain, and never plays out the melody. The mother staggers, and wanders blindly as though day and night were mingled into one, and struck through with preternatural influence of woe. But think not that God's silence is coldness or indifference! When Christ stood by the dead, the silence of tears interpreted His sympathy more wonderfully than even that voice which afterwards called back the footsteps of the brother from the grave, and planted them in life again! When birds are on the nest, preparing to bring forth life, they never sing. God's stillness is full of brooding. Not one tear shall be shed by you that does not hang heavier at His heart than any world upon His hand!

Be not impatient of God. Your sorrow is a seed sown. Shall a seed come up in a day, or come up all in blossom when it does spring? Let God plant your sorrows, and water and till them according to His own husbandry. By and by, when you gather their fruit, it will be time to judge His mercy. Now, no affliction "for the present seemeth to be joyous, but grievous: nevertheless afterward it yieldeth the peaceable fruit of righteousness unto them which are exercised thereby." Trouble is like any other crop. It needs time for growing, for blossoming, and for fruiting.

"Songs of glory to my God
　In the desert shall be heard!
There is comfort in Thy rod,
　Power in Thy reproving word.
In a spirit all Thine own,
Make Thy hardest sayings known.
They will gird me with Thy strength,
Bear me all my journey's length;
Give me for the daily strife,
Joy, and health, and plenteous life.
Hid within for precious fruit,
Love shall take eternal root—
Love that in the Spirit lives;
Love that grows by all it gives.
'Neath a rule so firm to bless,
I shall learn Thy gentleness;
Shew it forth in all I do—
Making others feel it too."

A. L. W.

The Reason of Prayer.

Psalm lxxxix. 5–8.

"And the heavens shall praise thy wonders, O Lord: thy faithfulness also in the congregation of the saints. For who in the heaven can be compared unto the Lord? Who among the mighty can be compared unto the Lord? God is greatly to be feared in the assembly of the saints, and to be had in reverence of all them that are about him. O Lord God of hosts, who is a strong Lord like unto thee? or to thy faithfulness round about thee?"

Psalm xlvi. 1–5.

"God is our refuge and strength, a very present help in trouble. Therefore will not we fear, though the earth be removed, and though the mountains be carried into the midst of the sea; though the waters thereof roar and be troubled, though the mountains shake with the swelling thereof. Selah. There is a river, the streams whereof shall make glad the city of God, the holy place of the tabernacles of the Most High. God is in the midst of her; she shall not be moved: God shall help her, and that right early."

Daniel ii. 20–22.

"Blessed be the name of God for ever and ever: for wisdom and might are his: and he changeth the times and the seasons: he removeth kings, and setteth up kings: he giveth wisdom unto the wise, and knowledge to them that know understanding: he revealeth the deep and secret things: he knoweth what is in the darkness, and the light dwelleth with him."

Isaiah xxvi. 4.

"Trust ye in the Lord for ever: for in the Lord Jehovah is everlasting strength."

"God of my life, to Thee I call;
  Afflicted at Thy feet I fall;
  When the great water-floods prevail,
  Leave not my trembling heart to fail.

"Friend of the friendless and the faint!
  Where should I lodge my deep complaint?
  Where but with Thee, whose open door,
  Invites the helpless and the poor!

"Did ever mourner plead with Thee
  And Thou refuse that mourner's plea?
  Does not the word still fix'd remain,
  That none shall seek Thy face in vain?

"That were a grief I could not bear,
  Didst Thou not hear and answer prayer;
  But a prayer-hearing, answering God,
  Supports me under every load.

"Fair is the lot that's cast for me;
  I have an advocate with Thee;
  They whom the world caresses most,
  Have no such privilege to boast.

"Poor though I am, despised, forgot,
  Yet God, my God, forgets me not;
  And he is safe, and must succeed,
  For whom the Lord vouchsafes to plead."

COWPER.

The Reason of Prayer.

THE human mind tends to pass from one extreme of truth to the other. The mind of communities touches both extremities before it settles down at the intermediate point of truth. There is no great truth which, being pressed far enough in one direction, will not meet another bearing up against it from the opposite. There is, for instance, the truth of man's liberty; press it far enough, and it will be met and restrained by the equal truth of man's dependence. The truth of man's individuality; press it to a certain distance, and it will meet another truth, equally certain — man's associated life. There is the truth of the necessity of helping men, and the other truth, just as important, that if you help them you will destroy them; for there is nothing worse than help which impairs the disposition of men to help themselves, and nothing so bad as not to help them when they need help. There is also the doctrine of free agency, and the counter-doctrine of dependence upon God. There is no one great line of thought which, being pursued at length, does not meet another coming from the opposite; and a man's mind should stand at the centre of the wheel, and all truths should come to it from every side as the spokes of one great wheel.

It is on this account that men vibrate between two extremes; and only after wide investigation that they take in all truth.

Before men had learned much of the globe, and of physical laws, they were guided, in assigning causes for the effects which they witnessed, by their veneration and imagination. When the imagination, instead of reason, guides ignorant men, they are almost always wont to ascribe effects, whose causes are not visible, to spiritual influence, infernal or supernal. The progress of observation and investigation drives men from these superstitious notions, and one effect after another is wrested from the supposed agency of spirits, and becomes affixed to its natural cause. This was the case with celestial appearances—the comets, the Aurora Borealis. This was the case also in a great measure with diseases. It is not long since pestilences, plagues, and many special forms of disease, such as leprosy, and many varieties of convulsive disease which affected the nervous system, were regarded by the medical faculty, and by the Church itself, as the results of spiritual or supernatural causes. It is only since the art of printing that these notions have been in a measure done away. I remember, in my own day, very long sermons to prove that the cholera did not depend on natural agencies, but that God held it in his hand, and dropped it down upon the world.

There is no doubt that there are moral results to be wrought out by all these natural phenomena, but it was held that they were produced by preternatural means. It is not many ages since a man would have been expelled from any sound church if he did not believe that diseases resulted from the direct exercise of Divine power, instead of intermediate causation; and that healing was to be effected only through some form of spiritual incantation.

The same was true of the common events of familiar life. Men saw evidence of the agency of good and of bad spirits around them, at all times, and in every minute event. Since the world began this has been common; and it is no commoner now than ever before. Men have always been watching with superstitious fear, lest, some charm being forgotten, lurking mischief should gain advantage of them.

The growth of natural science has tended very much to sweep away such views; first, from philosophical minds; gradually as general information increased, from the minds of all well-informed common men: and now, in the immense progress of science and the diffusion of a knowledge of it among the common people, there is a very marked tendency to go to the opposite extreme, and not only to refer each special effect to a corresponding natural cause, but to deny that there are any effects which are the results of Divine volition. Some men are ready to say that all things are effects of physical causes, and that there is no immediate Divine volition exerted upon natural laws. This is as monstrous in science, as it is absurd in religion. If men take the premise that all effects to be expected in this world are provided for in organised natural laws, and that there are none which result from Divine efficiency they must go through with all the conclusions. They must hold that human intelligence is our only guide in this world, or, in other words, is the only God of natural powers; they must argue that no man will be helped in this world except so far as he helps himself, by finding out the paths of nature and walking in them—a falsehood which is all the worse because it is half true. For in making an axe, the head is of iron and the edge of steel; but the head is the larger and heavier part, while the edge is but a narrow strip. So with such a falsehood; the greater part of it is true, but this is made only to add weight and power to the cutting edge, which is false. They must declare that the belief in a special and particular providence is a superstition; that God works by laws, and that He never interferes with or uses them. They must believe that, consequently, prayer is a mere poetic exercise; good to those that like it, only because it reacts upon their feelings, and soothes and calms them. They must suppose that prayers which the heathen write, and which the wind offers up for them by turning a wheel, like a mill, are as effectual on the laws of nature as an humble Christian's prayer. They must hold that the doctrine of miracles is to be given up, as nothing but a superlative superstition. And for this matter, such men usually do teach that miracles always happened in dark ages, among ignorant men; that many of the same results can now be produced by scientific causes; and that a belief in them, as effects divinely produced, is unworthy of an enlightened philosopher.

I need not say how far men have drifted away from the New Testament who have reached this ground. Such a man is not only not a Christian, but whatever natural religion he may have, if he be consistent, he must reject the New Testament altogether, as an authoritative guide, and give himself up to nature and reason. For if there be one truth more especially taught in the Bible than another, it is the fact of God's activity and influence in human life. If there ever comes a day in which it can be shewn by science that there is no active interference of the Divine creative will in the special affairs of men, science in that day will demolish the New Testament. When it can be scientifically demonstrated that no more effects are wrought in this world by the intentional interposition of Divine volition, than those which fall out in the way of ordinary and unhelped natural causation, in that day, I am free to say, the New Testament will be overthrown. It will be regarded as an amiable book, but one whose doctrines have been refuted, and are passed away.

This doctrine of the presence and actual interference of God in the world, producing effects which would not have fallen out otherwise, is taught in the Bible as against idolatry, as against naturalism, (in the early chapters of John,) as the argument and foundation of prayer, of courage, of patience, and of hope, and as a special development, among others, of the incarnation of Christ to bring to light the reality of God, who wrought invisibly in life and nature, both before and since.

It is to be admitted that this globe and its inhabitants are included in a system of physical laws; that these are, in their nature, unchanged and unchangeable; that they are incapable of increase or decrease; that they are sufficient for all ordinary purposes of human life; that the welfare and happiness of men depend largely upon a wise employment of them; and that the progress of the race is largely to be effected by their wise application of them. Not only would I cast no obstacle in the way of scientific research, but I hail it as the great almoner of God's bounty. Men should be instructed to become better acquainted with the laws and influences which operate upon both the body and the mind, and upon the natural world. Men will never be as good Christians as they ought, until they know more perfectly how their bodies are put together, and what is in their own minds, and the natural laws of the one and of the other. Science is yet to interpret Scripture in many respects; and I am persuaded that all the most characteristic elements of revealed or inspired truth will in the end be corroborated, and not harmed, by the progress of natural science. I believe in everything that is true. I am not necessarily to believe in everything that pretends to be true; but when anything is proved, whatever it overturns, I am bound to it by the allegiance with which I am bound to God! He that denies the truth in or out of the Bible, denies God!

The progress of science lays a surer foundation for a belief in God's active interference in human affairs than has existed without it. When maturer fruits of investigation shall be had, there can be no doubt that science itself will establish our faith in prayer, in miracles, and in special providence.

There are respects in which natural laws are beyond the reach of all human interference and control. There are spheres in which light and heat cannot be touched and controlled. There are various attractions which perform in their own way their own work, beyond man's guidance or reach—such are the great laws which bind together the stellar universe. Great currents and passages of natural powers are put entirely beyond man's hand. But it is just as certain that there are, also, in God's system of nature, another class of laws which come close to us, and whose office is, or seems to be, to minister to human life. They are either modifications of great laws, or they are separate laws.

And in respect to these I affirm that they are not fructified, and do not perform their function, till they are controlled by human volition. God has made the agencies which concern human life to be of such a nature that the *human mind is necessary to the full development and greatest fruitfulness of natural laws.* It is supposed by many that a natural law is perfect in itself; whereas it is perfected, in many instances, only when it is permeated by human volition.

Electricity, for instance, plays a round of its own. It has its own pastures, and its own great running grounds. It performs a large function, unknown, beyond our reach, and without our knowledge. But so far as ordinary purposes of civilised life are concerned, electricity does nothing till we have taught it how to serve us; then it runs swifter races for human convenience than ever were run before. When the mind takes hold of it, electricity becomes a patient drudge;

so that we now work by lightning, which would never have done a single thing for us if it had not been harnessed by the human mind. But now, above the sea, and under the sea ere long, it shall carry the messages of nations, flashing from the East to the West, proclaiming war or heralding peace, and performing the great offices of civilisation. When man takes it by the head and says, "Receive my bridle," and throws over it the saddle, and says, "Take me for your rider," it becomes patient and submissive, and acknowledges man as its master.

Light performs a great amount of work,—whether we are waking or sleeping; in its vast journeys through the universe—in its sun-flashes and moon-reflections; but man's mind seizes this law, and does what Phæton could not, *drives* it. We have it in our dwelling. We make it work along our coasts. We divide it, and set it at work in the garden and on the farm. We give it the power of a living pencil, and make it draw artists' pictures. And yet we are in the midst of a carping set of philosophers who say that we can obey natural laws, but cannot control them. We do control them.

Water has a certain round of grand effects, and these are performed whether a creature looks on or not. The ocean never asks man what it may do with its own waves and upon its own domain! The old Polar Sea — the only mystery now left among the oceans of the globe — has rolled for ages, by day and night, by summer and winter, with no eye to watch it — except from above! That mighty unexplored wilderness of mysterious water! — it does what it will, and is not dependent upon man. But water *is* dependent upon him for doing many things which it never could do otherwise. While it works in nature and on the globe, it is not subject to his will; but when it works for human life it immediately becomes his disciple. Man seizes the laws, and canals shoot forth, mills live, irrigation turns barren heaths to gardens, tides dig out channels, and the patient hydrostatic pump drives down to her element the vast Leviathan. Water could do none of these things without man's help. The things which natural laws can do without human volition are not so many, nor are they more wonderful than the things which they do only by the lifegiving touch of man's mind.

Heat, in the sun, produces the seasons. How vast is the great fire-place of the universe! Yet compare it with the sphere in which fire works under the dominion of man — in the forge, in the furnace, over the blow-pipe, serving the domestic range, warming the house, and pouring summer throughout the year within the dwellings!

Look at nature's fruits. There is but a *beginning* in natural fruits, and they never, when left to nature alone, reach beyond that point. When a man finds a crab-apple in the woods, he would not willingly find it more than once; yet, brought to his own orchard, it becomes a fine fruit. But did nature make the pippin? Nature had been trying her hand for years and years, and had never been able to get beyond the crab-apple. Man says to her, " You are a bungling apprentice; *I* will make you a journeyman." Nature can make iron, but she never made a sword. She never made a jack-knife, a steam-engine, a knife and fork— nothing but bare, cold, dead iron.

Now, is this a course of specious metaphysical reasoning? Is not this truth reasonable? Are not these facts alleged conclusive? And if they be true, what is the result? Nature has a certain crude, general function which natural laws perform of themselves, without any regard to men. But these laws are made to be vitalised and directed to a higher development by the control of the human mind and will. The laws of the globe are to be taken hold of by man's will, as really as the laws of the body are. The secondary effects of natural laws are just as much a part of their nature as the primary, and are of equal importance. In fact, it is these that constitute the elements of civilisation. While natural laws, in a certain way, influence and control men, yet they are, in the effects which they produce, just as much controlled by man, and just as dependent on him. If nature should abandon men, *they* would die, and *it* would become poverty-stricken. Let nature forget us, and the heart would cease to beat. The pulsations of endless electrical currents would cease. On the other hand, let man forget nature, and the city would crumble, and go back to a wilderness; the garden which had grown up from a thistle-ground, would return to its native condition; cultivated seeds would shrink back to their original poverty; and all domestic animals would rebound to their wild state. Nature needs man to keep her at work.

It is this view that settles all questions about man's necessity to obey. God has not put us before nature to make us only its pupil, but also its master. We are not alone to look up and take, but to look down and control. We are not only to obey, but also to rule. We are to obey for the sake of ruling. The whole talk about the absolute and inflexible government of natural law has no foundation except in fool's brains. It is a divided empire, and man's part is more than nature's. When God made man, He made more of nature in Him than He did in all the rest of the world besides!

The question now arises, Is there a moral or scientific probability that God ever produces results by natural laws in this world which otherwise would not have been produced? If we drive natural laws, cannot God do it? I hold, because the Bible teaches it, and now I hold it more because nature and science teach it, that there are millions of results that never would have fallen out in the course of nature that are now continually happening on account of God's special mercy. The doctrine of a special providence is this: God administers natural laws — of the mind, of the body, and the outward world — so as to produce effects which they never would have done of themselves. Man can do this, and why not God? By a wise use of natural laws, man can make the difference between comfort and discomfort. He can till the farm, and make the seasons serve him. He can take natural laws, and gird himself about with them, so that they shall make him rich, and wise, and strong. Men can do it for themselves — why cannot God do it for them? Men can do it for their children, for their neighbours' children, for scores and hundreds of persons. A farmer that administers his estate wisely, will have enough, not only for himself, but for others. His children will be fed, the neighbourhood supplied, and the veins of commerce swollen by the overplus of his sagacity. A man can say to the light, to the water, to the seasons, "I will, by you, make a special providence for this whole town," and he can do it; for if he falls back, there will not be abundance, but if he goes forward there will be. That is not all. A man may be put at a point where — as Napoleon was, or Wellington in Spain, or Sir John Moore in the north of Portugal, or Clive in India — he can make a special providence for a nation, for a race, for an age, for one land, or for the globe. Now, God can do a great deal more than man, and a great deal better. Is there any objection to such a doctrine?

In regard to the doctrine of prayer, many men say, "Do you suppose that God will make any difference whether you pray or not?" The reply is, that

God can if He chooses. But whether He will or not, depends very much on how I pray, and what I pray for. I can give my boy a book or a bow every day in the year, but whether I will or not is another thing. God will not do for men what men can do for themselves. Nor will He do for them at present what they, after a proper course of development, will by and by be able to do for themselves. But a man has a right to go up along the path of his weakness, and say, "I have done what I could; now hear my prayer, and do for me what I cannot do for myself." And if it is a thing that is needed, God will answer the prayer. For He loves to give needed things better than earthly parents love to give good gifts to their children. Suppose you have been travelling on the railway with your child, and it ha e shall restless with fatigue. Its re᳐u prayer, or broken by night-travelli- miracles; but all gry and asks for foo be solved, and their .way.

snow lies across the track, and the train cannot go on. It waits. Anybody would feel pity for such a child — even if it were a stranger's! But how much more if it were his own? And if it be my child, and says, "Pa, water, water," it cuts me to the heart to hear it! But by and by, with double and treble elements of iron, the track is opened, the way is cleared, and we are hurried on to the next station. The first bolt I make is into the hotel; for I am hungry, not for myself, but for the child; and I break through the crowd back again to the train with bread in my hands for the child. Ah, do you suppose the bread is half so sweet to his mouth as to my eyes that watch his eager eating? But this is God's figure, and not mine. He declares that He is more willing to give good gifts
In ₥ that ask Him, than parents are
many men ᵇₑir children.
God will make ₑ prayed on this princi-
you pray or not?" ᵣ prayer unanswered?

Not prayer for amusement; for some men pray, who begin with Adam, and come leisurely down all the way through to "Thy kingdom come," and then wind up with the "power and glory, for ever and ever. Amen." That is not prayer; or at least it is not such praying as will be answered. But did you ever, under the pressure of a real want, go to God and say, "Thou, Father, canst help me; give me thine aid," and not have your prayer answered? Glorious old Martin Luther knew how to pray. He used to take one of God's promises, and laying it down, would say, "Now, Lord, here is Thy word! If Thou dost not keep it, I will never believe Thee again." This may be called audacious, but it was not audacity in such a Christian as Luther.

What is needed is, that we should take a larger and broader faith, and we shall then have no difficulty with prayer, or special providences, or miracles; but all their problems will be solved, and their mysteries cleared away.

"O Lord! how happy should we be
   If we could cast our care on Thee,
      If we from self could rest;
   And feel at heart that One above
   In perfect wisdom, perfect love,
      Is working for the best.

"How far from this our daily life!
   Ever disturbed by anxious strife,
      By sudden wild alarms;
   Oh, could we but relinquish all
   Our earthly props, and simply fall
      On Thy almighty arms!

"Could we but kneel and cast our load,
   E'en while we pray, upon our God,
      Then rise with lighten'd cheer;
   Sure that the Father, who is nigh,
   To still the famish'd raven's cry,
      Will hear, in that we fear.

"We cannot trust Him as we should,
   So chafes fallen nature's restless mood
      To cast its peace away;
   Yet birds and flowerets round us preach—
   All, all the present evil teach,
      Sufficient for the day.

"Lord, make these faithless hearts of ours
   Such lessons learn from birds and flowers,
      Make therefrom self to cease;
   Leave all things to a Father's will,
   And taste, before Him lying still,
      E'en in affliction, peace."

The Great Exemplar.

HEBREWS ii. 16–18.

"For verily he took not on him the nature of angels; but he took on him the seed of Abraham. Wherefore in all things it behoved him to be made like unto his brethren, that he might be a merciful and faithful high priest in things pertaining to God, to make reconciliation for the sins of the people. For in that he himself hath suffered being tempted, he is able to succour them that are tempted."

HEBREWS iii. 1, 2.

"Wherefore, holy brethren, partakers of the heavenly calling, consider the Apostle and High Priest of our profession, Christ Jesus; who was faithful to him that appointed him, as also Moses was faithful in all his house."

HEBREWS iv. 15.

"For we have not an High Priest which cannot be touched with the feeling of our infirmities; but was in all points tempted like as we are, yet without sin."

JOHN xvi. 23, 24.

"Verily, verily, I say unto you, Whatsoever ye shall ask the Father in my name, he will give it you. Hitherto have ye asked nothing in my name: ask, and ye shall receive, that your joy may be full."

1 JOHN ii. 1.

"And if any man sin, we have an advocate with the Father, Jesus Christ the righteous."

"O Jesu, teach me like Thyself to fly
This poisonous world, and all its charms defy.
Give me devotion which shall never tire;
Fix'd contemplation which my love may fire;
A heavenly tincture in my whole discourse,
A fervent zeal which may my prayers enforce;
Of heavenly joys a sweet foretasting view,
That I on earth may only heaven pursue."

BISHOP KEN.

"Here in Thy gracious hands I fall,
    To Thee I cling with faith's embrace;
O righteous Sovereign, hear my call,
    And turn, oh, turn, to me in grace!
For through Thy sorrows I am just,
    And guilt no more in me is found;
Thus reconciled, my soul is bound
To Thee in endless love and trust.

"Yes, yes, to Thee my soul would cleave,
    Oh choose it, Saviour, for Thy throne!
Couldst Thou in love to me once leave
    The glory that was all Thine own,
So honour Thou my life and heart,
    That Thou mayst find a heaven in me;
And when this house decay'd shall be,
Then grant the heaven where now Thou art."

LYRA GERMANICA.

The Great Exemplar.

LEAVING the crowded shore, the thronged highway, and, crossing the turfy fields, Christ came to the edges of the mountains. His pulse throbbed and his breath quickened as He clomb, as ours do when we climb. The sparrow, not knowing its Creator and Protector, flew away from His coming. His form cast its shadow, as He passed, over bush, and flower, and grass, and they knew not that their Maker overshadowed them. Sounds grew fainter behind Him. Those who had followed Him, one by one, dropped off, and the last eye that looked after Him had lost His form amid the wavering leaves, and was withdrawn. He was in the mountain, and alone. The day was passing. The last red light followed

Him, and stained the air of the forest with ruddy hues. At length the sun went down, and it was twilight in the mountains, though bright yet in the open field. But when it was twilight in the field, it was already dark on the mountain. The stars were coming forward and filling the heavens.

No longer drawn outward by the wants of the crowd, what were the thoughts of such a soul? And what were the prayers? Even if Christ were but a man, such an errand, and of such a man, would be sublime! But how foolish are all words which would approach the grandeur of Christ's solitude upon the mountain, if we regard Him as very God, though incarnated, communing with His coequal Father!

What was the varied prayer? What tears were shed, what groans were breathed, what silent yearnings, what voiceless utterances of desire, no man may know. Walking to and fro, or sitting upon some fallen rock, or prostrate in overpowering emotion, the hours passed on until morning dawned. When He went down to His disciples, they neither inquired nor did He speak of His mountain watch.

If prayer be the communion of the soul with God, it is but a little part of it that can be uttered in words; and still less of it that will take form of words in the presence of others. Of outward wants, of outward things, of one's purely earthly estate, we can speak freely. But of the soul's inward life — of its struggles with itself, its hopes, yearnings, griefs, loves, joys, of its very personality — it is reserved, and to such a degree, that there can be no prayer expressive of the inward life, until we have entered into the closet, and shut to the door. Every Christian, whose life has developed itself into great experience of secret prayer, knows that the hidden things of the closet transcend all uttered prayer as much in depth, richness, and power, as they do in volume and space.

Sometimes we mourn the loss of old books in ancient libraries; we marvel what more the world would have had if the Alexandrian library had not perished; we regret the decay of parchments, the rude waste of monks with their stupid palimpsests. We sorrow for the lost arts, and grieve that the fairest portions of Grecian art lie buried from research; that the Parthenon should come down within two hundred years of our time, with its wealth of magnificence, a voice in stone from the old world to the new, and yet perish almost before our eyes!

But when one reflects upon the secret history which has transpired in men's thoughts, and that the noblest natures have been they whose richest experiences could never have been drawn forth through the pen, or recorded in books — but have found utterance through prayer, and before the conscious glory of the Invisible Presence — I am persuaded that the silent literature of the closet is infinitely more wonderful, in every attribute of excellence, than all that has been sung in song, or recorded in literature, or lost in all the concussions of time. If rarest classical fragments, the perished histories and poets of every people, could be revived, they would be as nothing in comparison with the effusions of the closet, could they be gathered and recorded.

The noblest natures, it is, that resort to this study. The rarest inspiration rests upon them. Flying between the heavens and the earth, with winged faith, they reach out into glories which do not descend to the lower spheres of thought.

How many souls, so large and noble that they rose up in those days of persecution, and left home and love for the faith of Christ, and went to the wilderness and dwelt therein, gave forth in prayer their whole life! Doubtless their daily prayers were rich and deep in spiritual life. But there are peculiar days to all — days of vision — days when we see all human life as in a picture, and all future life as in a vision; and when the reason, the imagination, the affections, and the experiences of life are so tempered together that we consciously live more in an hour than at other times in months. Every man has his mountains of transfiguration, and sees and talks with the revealed and radiant dead. In such experiences, what must have been the wonders of prayer, when the noblest natures — rich in all goodness, deeply cultured in knowledge, refined in all taste, and enriched in pure lives, but driven out among the wild shaking leaves of the wilderness for their faith's sake — poured out their whole soul before God; their conscious weakness and sinfulness, their yearnings and trials, their hopes and strivings, their sense of this life and their view of the other, their longing for God's Church on earth and their prospect of the glorified Church in heaven! What if some listener had made haste to put down the prayers of Luther, with all his strong crying and tears, if that had been possible! How many noble natures gave up to celibacy and virginity the wondrous treasures of multitudinous affections. And when at periods of heart-swellings, in hours when the secret tide set in upon men from the eternal ocean, and carried them upon mighty longings and yearnings towards God, before whom they poured forth in mingled sobs and words those affections which were meant to be eased in the love-relations of life, but which, hindered and choked, found tumultuous vent in mighty prayer to God!

Consider what mothers' hearts have always been. How many thousand thousands of them have watched day and night over the cradle till the body failed and the spirit waxed even keener; and with what wondrous gushes of words, such as would disdain to be called eloquence, have they besought God, with every persuasion, for the life of the child! We judge these things by our own experience. All the words that were ever spoken, and all the thoughts that we have conceived, are unfit to bear up the skirt of those prayers, which burst, without words, right out of our hearts, for the life of dying children!

Consider what a heavenly wonder must be the Book of Prayer that lies before God! For groans are interpreted there. Mute joys gain tongue before God. Unutterable desires, that go silently up from the heart, burst forth into divine pleadings when, touched by the Spirit, their imprisoned nature comes forth! Could thoughts or aspirations be made visible, could they assume a form that befitted their nature, what an endless procession would be seen going towards the throne of God, day and night! Consider the wrestlings of all the wretched, the cry of orphans, the ceaseless pleadings of the bereaved, and of those fearing bereavement; the prayer of trust betrayed, of hope darkened, of home deserted, of joy quenched; the prayers of faithful men from dungeons and prison-houses; the prayers of slaves, who found man, law, and the Church twined around and set against them, and had no way left to look but upward towards God! The hearts of men by myriads have been pressed by the world as grapes are trodden in a wine-press, and have given forth a heavenly wine. Beds of long-lingering sickness have learned such thoughts of resignation, and such patient trust and joy, that the heavenly book is bright with the footprints of their prayers! The very silence of sickness is often more full of richest thoughts than all the books of earth have ever been!

"And when he had taken the book, the four beasts and four and twenty elders fell down before the Lamb, having every one of them harps, and golden vials full of odors, *which are the prayers of saints.*" And the other magnificence of the scene one may read in the fifth chapter of that gorgeous book of divine pictures, the Revelation of St. John! How remarkable would it seem, if it were revealed to us that there dwelt in the air a race of fine and fairy spirits, whose work it was to watch all flowers of the earth, and catch their perfumed breath and preserve it in golden vials for heavenly use! But how much more grand is the thought that, all over the earth, God's angels have caught the heart's breath, its prayers, and love, and that in heaven they are before God like precious odors poured from golden vases by saintly hands!

The influences which are at work upon the soul in such a covert as the closet are not like the coarse stimulants of earthly thought. It is no fierce rivalry, no conflict for victory, no hope of praise or hunger of fame, that throw lurid light upon the mind. The soul rises to its highest nature, and meets the influence that rests upon it from above. What is the depth of calmness, what is the vision of faith, what is the rapture, the ecstasy of love, the closet knows more grandly than any other place of human experience!

"Not seldom, clad in radiant vest,
　　Deceitfully goes forth the morn;
Not seldom, evening in the west,
　　Sinks smilingly forsworn.

"The smoothest seas will sometimes prove
　　To the confiding bark untrue;
And if she trusts the stars above,
　　They can be treacherous too.

"The umbrageous oak, in pomp outspread,
　　Full oft when storms the welkin rend,
Draws lightning down upon the head
　　It promised to defend.

"But Thou art true, incarnate Lord!
　　Who didst vouchsafe for man to die;
Thy smile is sure, Thy plighted word
　　No change can falsify.

"I bent before Thy gracious throne,
　　And asked for peace with suppliant knee;
And peace was given,—nor peace alone,
　　But faith sublimed to ecstasy!"
　　　　　　　　　　　　WORDSWORTH.

Come Boldly.

Hebrews x. 19–23.

"Having therefore, brethren, boldness to enter into the holiest by the blood of Jesus, by a new and living way, which he hath consecrated for us, through the vail, that is to say, his flesh; and having an High Priest over the house of God; let us draw near with a true heart in full assurance of faith, having our hearts sprinkled from an evil conscience, and our bodies washed with pure water. Let us hold fast the profession of our faith without wavering; (for he is faithful that promised.)"

1 John v. 14, 15.

"And this is the confidence that we have in him, that, if we ask anything according to his will, he heareth us; and if we know that he hear us, whatsoever we ask, we know that we have the petitions that we desired of him."

Psalm lxii. 7, 8.

"In God is my salvation and my glory: the rock of my strength, and my refuge, is in God. Trust in him at all times; ye people, pour out your heart before him: God is a refuge for us. Selah."

Hebrews iv. 15, 16.

"For we have not an High Priest which cannot be touched with the feeling of our infirmities; but was in all points tempted like as we are, yet without sin. Let us therefore come boldly unto the throne of grace, that we may obtain mercy, and find grace to help in time of need."

John xiv. 14.

"If ye shall ask any thing in my name, I will do it."

"Come, then, let us hasten yonder;
      Here let all,
      Great and small,
Kneel in awe and wonder.
Love Him who with love is yearning;
      Hail the Star
      That from far
Bright with hope is burning!

"Ye who pine in weary sadness,
      Weep no more,
      For the door
Now is found of gladness:
Cling to Him, for He will guide you
      Where no cross,
      Pain or loss,
Can again betide you.

"Hither come, ye heavy-hearted;
      Who for sin,
      Deep within,
Long and sore have smarted;
For the poison'd wounds you're feeling
      Help is near,
      One is here
Mighty for their healing!

"Hither come, ye poor and wretched;
      Know His will
      Is to fill
Every hand outstretched;
Here are riches without measure,
      Here forget
      All regret,
Fill your hearts with treasure."

"Come Boldly to the Throne."

MANY passages of the Scripture are like hundreds of wayside flowers, which for months and years are unnoticed by us, simply because we have been accustomed from our childhood to see them without stooping to pluck or to examine them. Many of the homeliest flowers would appear transcendently beautiful if we would take the trouble to study them minutely, to magnify their parts, and to bring out their constituent elements. And so, we were taught to read the Bible so early, in the family and in the village school, and we have so often and often walked along the chapters, that we have beaten a dusty path in them, and some of their most precious and beautiful things are neither precious nor beautiful to us, simply because we look *at* them and not *into* them. Many parts of the Bible may be compared to those exquisite creations of art which are sometimes found in old cathedrals; they have collected dust and grime and weather-stains; hundreds of persons go past them every day, never cleansing them, never restoring feature nor colour, nor bringing out the artist's embodied thought, so that they are quite unconscious, till they see them restored in the picture of some book, or till some enthusiastic Ruskin brings them out, and teaches us how beautiful are the things that we have slighted as uncomely. So the Scriptures are often overlaid, and, frequently, some of the passages that really are the most resplendent are those which seem only common and ordinary.

Just such a passage is to be found in the third chapter of the Ephesians, in which Paul says: " For this cause I bow my knees unto the Father of our Lord

Jesus Christ, of whom the whole family in heaven and earth is named, that he would grant you, according to the riches of his glory, to be strengthened with might by his Spirit in the inner man; that Christ may dwell in your hearts by faith; that ye, being rooted and grounded in love, may be able to comprehend with all saints what is the breadth, and length, and depth, and height; and to know the love of Christ, which passeth knowledge, that ye might be filled with all the fulness of God." What a passage is this! But this is not all. This is a prayer; and the apostle having made a prayer which few men can climb, takes a still higher flight, and says: "Now unto Him that is able to do exceeding abundantly above all that we ask or think, according to the power that worketh in us, unto him be glory in the church by Christ Jesus throughout all ages, world without end. Amen."

These words are, throughout,

lime strain against despondency. Paul was in prison. "For this cause," the chapter begins, "I Paul, the prisoner." His design was to present such a view of the fulness of God's heart, and of the grandeur of His administration, as should be an offset against any possible weakness, disaster, overthrow, or trouble in life, to Christians, both as individuals and as churches.

It is a presentation of God in such a light as shall enkindle praise. "Now unto Him"—the very words indicate the mood of devout ascription. He would excite joy and adoration in view of God's royal generosity and large-heartedness. The Divine generosity is measured not only by our wants, but by our thoughts and desires above our wants, and it equals and transcends both. He is "able to do exceeding abundantly above all that we ask or think."

The word "abundance" expresses the more than enough. "Enough" is a measuring word. It is the complete filling of a given measure. It satisfies the demand. It just equals the want. But "abundance" is something over and above. It is "enough and to spare." A handful of berries or dried fruits given to a pilgrim who is ready to perish of hunger, might be enough to stay his strength and satisfy his appetite; but if, instead of this, the kind heart of sympathy should throw open the garden gate and the orchard, and say to him, "Go in, pluck and eat," even when the lively appetite had sated itself upon the nearest fruits, there would still be on every bush and bough, in hundreds of rows and ranks, throughout the garden and the orchard, multitudes of kinds and the utmost abundance in quantity, of sweet and delicious fruits, which he could not begin to eat nor even to taste. In the one case he would have simply "enough," in the other "abundance."

Saith the armourer, "I will not be

wasteful," and he uses steel with an economic eye in forging the blade; and the smith measures his iron for each purpose. So he that pays a debt at the bank lays down the exact amount to a penny, but no more. The apothecary takes the physician's prescription, and weighing it out, allows himself no generosity in measuring the ingredients of the medicine, but puts it up by drachms and scruples with rigid exactitude. God does not so measure in creating, or in sustaining, or in administering. On the other hand, the thought of God which the apostle conveys, is that of a Being of magnificent richness, who does everything in overmeasure. The whole Divine character and administration, the whole conception of God set forth in the Bible and in nature, is of a Being of magnificence and munificence, of abundance and superabundance. Did you ever take the trouble to look at a lazy bank that bears nothing for itself? It has no trees growing out of it for grateful shade, and no vines with cooling clusters, and no grass which herds may browse upon, and no flowers that lap over it, and yet the hair of ten thousand reeds will be combed upon its brow, and it will be spotted and patched with moss, of ten thousand patterns of exquisite beauty, so that any artist who, in all his life, should produce one such thing, would make himself a master-spirit in art, and immortal in fame. God's least thought in the barrenest places of nature is more prolific than man's greatest abundance. God is a Being of great thoughts, great feelings, great actions. Whenever He does anything, He never does it narrowly, certainly not meanly. He never cuts out such a pattern, and then works up to it with even edge. He is a royal Creator, who says to the earth, "Let it swarm abundantly," and to the sea, "Let it be endlessly filled." He touches the sand of the shore, and it stands forth as a representative of the abundance of His thought.

He spreads out the heavens, and no man can count the fiery stars. He orders the seasons, and they all speak in their endless procession of this one thought of God—His everlasting abundance!

But "abundance" is a relative word. What is abundance for a wayfarer is not abundance for a shepherd. What was abundant for a nomad, a wandering shepherd, would not be for a settled farmer, with crops and stock, with barns and houses. But what is abundant for a farmer, would not be for a merchant; and what is abundant for a merchant would be very sparse and scant for a prince; and even among princes there is great difference of degree. The abundance of a German prince would be poverty for the court of the royal Czar. Now, put the word, with its relative and increased significance, upon God. Divine abundance! The fulness of God! It is not in the power of man to conceive it! If God might be supposed to have worked narrowly anywhere it would be on the earth, His footstool. But the earth is infinitely full of God's thought. And yet, great as the earth is absolutely, it is relatively little, and all symbols and figures drawn from earthly things stop on this side of the Divine idea of abundance.

But the apostle says, " Now unto Him that is able to do *exceeding* abundantly." What a vision he must have had! How grandly in that moment did the divine though rise before his enrapt mind, when he so linked words together, seeking by combinations to express what no one word had the power to flash forth. He could not by the mightiest single word express his own thought and feeling, and so he joined golden word with golden word, as if he fain would encompass it with a chain!

But Paul employs a measure of comparison even over and above all this: " above all that we can ask or think." That is, above the measure of all human aspirations. How much can a man ask or think? When the deepest convictions of sin are upon him, in his hour of deep despondency, in critical and trying circumstances, when fears come upon his soul as storms came on the lake of Galilee, consider how much a man would then ask, and how much more think! Or, when love swells every vein in his soul, and makes life as full as mountains make the streams in spring-time, and hope is the sun by day and the moon by night, in those gloriously elate hours in which he seems no longer fixed to space and time, but, springing as if the body were forgotten by the soul, wings his way through the realms of aspiration and conception, consider how much a man then *thinks!*

All books are dry and tame compared with that great unwritten book prayed in the closet. The prayers of exiles! The prayers of martyrs! The prayers of missionaries! The prayers of the

Waldenses! The prayers of the Albigenses! The prayers of the Covenanters! The sighs, the groans, the inarticulate cries of suffering men, whom tyrants have buried alive in dungeons — whom the world may forget, but God never! If some angel, catching them as they were uttered, should drop them down from heaven, what a liturgy they would make! Can any epic equal those unwritten words that pour into the ear of God out of the heart's fulness!

Still more, what epic can equal the unspoken words, that never find the lip, but go up to heaven in unutterable longings and aspirations! Words are but the bannerets of a great army; thoughts are the main body of the footmen. Words show here and there a little gleam in the air, but the great multitude of thoughts march unseen below. Words cannot follow aspiration even in its tamer flights; still less when it takes wings and flies upward, borne by the breath of God's Holy Spirit. I see the gulls from my window day by day, making circuits against the north wind. They mount up above the masts of vessels in the stream, and then suddenly drop almost to the water's edge, flying first in one direction and then in another, that they may find some eddy unobstructed by that steady-blowing blast, until they turn finally with the wind, and then like a gleam of light their white wings flash down the bay faster than any eye can follow them! So when men's aspirations are borne by some divine wind towards heaven, they take swift upward flight, and no words can follow them!

Consider what a soul thinks in yearnings for itself, and in yearnings even more for others; what a saint thinks in hours of vision and aspiration, when he reflects how all his life long, through good report and through evil report, through manifold trials of temper, of mind, of feeling, in his family and out, the hand of God has led him every day, and his cup has been filled to overflowing; consider what a dying man thinks in view of death and of judgment and immortality awaiting him beyond the grave! What wonderful thoughts! What wonderful feelings! And yet the apostle's measurement is more than all these, for he says: "Now unto him that is able to do exceeding abundantly above all that we ask or think!" How true it is that God's riches are unsearchable!

This is the idea of God toward which men ought always to repent. It is sometimes supposed that repentance is drudgery. It is drudgery in a mean man, but in no one else. There is a kind of mean repentance that needs to be repented of. But when a child knows that his misconduct has really hurt a loving parent, the child is more pained than the parent. When a noble spirit has done wrong to a friend, through some misunderstanding that has sprung up between them, such man *demands* the liberty of restoring a himself more than the other demands that he shall restore himself. When we have injured a friend, it is our privilege to make it good. It is necessary to our thought of manhood that we should repair a wrong done. How much more when we have wronged Christ, our Elder Brother, our Redeemer, our Friend, our joy and our comfort, should we make haste to repent — not as a duty, but as a sweet privilege; not with the thought that our repentance is a necessity made so by Him, but made necessary by our own honour and conscience? To sit down in a corner, and to cry so much, and to feel so bad, and to mourn so long, is not repentance. True repentance springs out of the most generous feelings of a Christian heart. It is a man's better nature triumphing over his lower and meaner. A Christian should never say, "I must repent," but, "Let me repent." It is the goodness of God that should lead us to repentance, not His justice and His terrors. Many persons suppose that God sits on the throne of the heavens as storm-clouds that float in summer skies, full of bolts and lightnings; and they are either repelled, or they think they must come to Him under the covert of some excuse. But repentance ought to lead us to God as toward light, toward summer, toward heaven made glorious with His presence, toward His everlasting goodness. His eye is not dark with vengeance, nor His heart turbulent with wrath, and to repent toward His justice and vindictiveness must be always from a lower motive than toward His generosity and His love.

It is with such a conception of God that Christians should come before Him with their wants. It is a glorious comfort that God's love is as infinite as His power. We are all apt to think of His *power* as infinite, and we call Him omnipotent; but we too often forget that His *love* also is infinite. It has no end, no measure, no bound. A man's generous feelings are often like the buds at this season of the year — wrapped up in coverings to keep them from the selfishness and coldness of the world. By and by they may burst out and bloom, yet now they are circumscribed. But we do not have in ourselves the measure of the love of God. How base it is, then, when we have some gift to ask of Him, to go with shrinking confidence and with piteous look, as though there were need of importunity. Is it possible, if with men "it is more blessed to give than to receive," that it is not infinitely more with God? To a true Christian heart, next to the pain of being unable to do for those who are in want, is the pleasure of being approached by them, when we have it in our power to help them. Is it not the same, and in an infinitely higher degree with God? The happiest being in the universe is God, because He has an infinite desire of benevolence, and infinite means of gratifying it. There is with Him no limitation, either of heart or hand.

Such a view of God, habitually taken, will deliver us from unworthy fears, and will inspire in us great boldness of approach, and access with confidence, unto the throne of His grace. It will tend to comfort Christians who are in despondency respecting their rectitude through life, their victory in death, and their glorification in heaven; for these things are thus made to stand, not in a Christian's feeble desire for them, but on God's infinite desire and abundant grace. When stars, first created, start forth upon their vast circuits, not knowing their way, if they were conscious and sentient, they might feel hopeless of maintaining their revolutions and orbits, and might despair in the face of coming ages! But, without hands or arms, the sun holds them! Without cords or bands, the solar king drives them unharnessed on their mighty rounds without a single misstep, and will bring them in the end to their bound, without a single wanderer. But the sun is but a thing, itself driven and held; and shall not He, who created the heavens, and appointed all the stars to their places, and gave the sun his power, be able to hold you by the attraction of His heart, the strength of His hands, and the omnipotence of His affectionate will?

It is this view of God that the apostles taught. We read it on every page of Paul and Peter and James and John — everywhere in the New Testament. What was the beginning? "Peace on earth, good-will to men!" And what was the last word that was heard ringing through the air before the message was sealed, and the vision failed? "The Spirit and the bride say, Come; let him that heareth say, Come; let him that is athirst come; and whosoever will, let him come and take of the water of life freely."

Whosoever will! That is the Alpha and the Omega! That is the beginning and the ending! That is the offer; that is the promise. And what shall be the response of every Christian heart, if it be not those final and sublimest words of the great Revelator, "Even so, Lord Jesus, come quickly!"

"All eyes do wait on Thee, O Lord,
  Who keepest us from dearth,
Who scatterest rich supplies abroad
  For all the wants of earth ;
Thou openest oft Thy bounteous hand,
And all in sea, and air, and land,
  Are fill'd with food and mirth.

"Thy thoughts are good, and Thou art kind,
  E'en when we think it not ;
How many an anxious, faithless mind
  Sits grieving o'er its lot,
And frets and pines by day and night,
As God had lost it out of sight,
  And all its wants forgot !

"Ah, no ! God ne'er forgets His own,
  His heart is far too true ;
He ever seeks their good alone,
  His love is daily new ;
And though thou deem that things go ill,
Yet He, in all He doeth, still
  Is holy, just, and true.

"The Lord to them is ever nigh
  Who truly keep His word ;
Whene'er in faith to Him they cry,
  Their prayer is surely heard.
He knoweth well who love Him well—
His love shall yet their clouds dispel,
  And grant the hope deferr'd."

LYRA GERMANICA.

The Scope of Prayer.

PHILIPPIANS iv. 6.

"Be careful for nothing; but in every thing by prayer and supplication with thanksgiving let your requests be made known unto God."

JAMES v. 16.

"Pray one for another, that ye may be healed. The effectual fervent prayer of a righteous man availeth much."

ISAIAH xliii. 25, 26.

"I, even I, am he that blotteth out thy transgressions for mine own sake, and will not remember thy sins. Put me in remembrance: let us plead together: declare thou, that thou mayest be justified."

JOB v. 8–10.

"I would seek unto God, and unto God would I commit my cause: which doeth great things and unsearchable; marvellous things without number: who giveth rain upon the earth, and sendeth waters upon the fields."

PSALM cxxi.

"I will lift up mine eyes unto the hills, from whence cometh my help. My help cometh from the Lord, which made heaven and earth. He will not suffer thy foot to be moved: he that keepeth thee will not slumber. Behold, he that keepeth Israel shall neither slumber nor sleep. The Lord is thy keeper: the Lord is thy shade upon thy right hand. The sun shall not smite thee by day, nor the moon by night. The Lord shall preserve thee from all evil: he shall preserve thy soul. The Lord shall preserve thy going out and thy coming in from this time forth, and even for evermore."

"Art thou a pilgrim, and alone?
  Far from the home once call'd thine own?
  From friendship's faithful bosom wrested,
  In strangers' hands thy comforts vested,
  Thy life a cheerless winter day,
    Unlit by sunshine? Rise and pray!

"Smiled on thee once the bliss of earth,
  And glittering joys of transient worth?
  Hast thou adored some idol shrine,
  Or bent has many a knee at thine?
  Faded these creatures of a day,
    What hast thou left? Arise and pray!

"Or hast thou, driven by deepest woe,
  Thy soul's sure refuge learn'd to know?
  And every storm of life would meet
  Beneath the sheltering Mercy-Seat?
  Whether in youth or life's decay,
    Thy lot is blest—thou lovest to pray!

"But haply thou, even thou hast found
  Religion's consecrated ground
  With sorrows and with snares beset;
  Which, though the almighty Sufferer met
  To conquer, we must yet obey
    His welcome mandate—Rise and pray!

"Even should that direst hour be thine,
  When in the darkening heavens no sign
  Appears—but thou in combat fell,
  Must meet the adverse hosts of hell,
  Oh never cast the hope away,
    While thou canst lift thy heart to pray!

"With tears, with bitterest agony,
  The Saviour wrestled, soul! for thee
  Ere He could all-triumphant rise
  To plead the accepted sacrifice;
  So, till the world shall pass away,
    Shall stand His words—'Arise and pray!'"

E. M.

The Scope of Prayer.

ONE may perceive at a glance how exceedingly wide is the scope of prayer.

It will begin with a supplication for our temporal wants. These are first felt, and felt longest; and by the greatest number of the world felt chiefly. Next higher will come petitions for relief from trouble, for remedy, for shelter in danger. In this, too, the soul may exercise its own liberty; there are no metes nor bounds. Then, next, prayer is drawn forth by heart-sorrow. A wounded spirit, a bruised heart, naturally turns for confidence and soothing towards God. Its prayer may be supplication for help, or it may be only recitation for the sake of peace. Next, and far higher, prayer becomes the resource of a heart exercised for its own religious growth. It is the cry for help against temptation. It is the voice of confession. It is a recital of sins committed, and a plaint of sorrow for them. It is the soul's liberty to go to its Father with all its growing pains, its labour and travail in spiritual things. Prayer, also, to one who lives in the daily service of God, oftentimes takes the form of simple communion, the spreading out of our life to one who is worthy, whom we love and trust, not for the sake of any special advice, nor for the sake of special help, but for the heart-rest which there is in the thing itself. For none love confidences so much as they who rarely have them. None love to speak so much, when the mood of speaking comes, as they who are naturally taciturn. None love to lean and recline entirely upon another so much as strong natures that ordinarily do not lean at all. And so the heart that goes shaded and shut, that hides its thoughts and dreads the knowledge of men's eyes, flings itself wide open to the eye of God.

Thus, I have sat down within the green wood, and while men were passing, feet tramping, and voices shouting, everything in the boughs and among the leaves hid itself. But after the noise had died out, sitting still and motionless as the tree I leaned against, I have heard a sweet note sounded near me; then a brief response from yonder bush; a bird had hopped down upon the leaves, squirrels had come forth lithe and merry; and in a few moments all the secrets and confidences of sylvan shades were revealed to me. And thus it is in the soul that shuts itself and holds its peace while the world is near, but grows securer in silence of contemplation, and lets out its gentle thoughts and whispering joys, its hopes or sad fears, unto the listening ear and before the kindly eye of God!

But in souls which have caught something of the beauty of the divine life, prayer in many of its moods becomes more than this. There are times of yearning and longing, far beyond the help of the most hopeful. There is a prayer which is the voice of the soul pleading its birthright, crying out for its immortality; it is heavenly homesickness!

There are times, too, of great joys and gratitudes—times in which nothing is so congenial as to express the soul's thoughts of gladness, its spiritual gaiety. In some lovely morning of spring, after days of storm have made nature mute—when the bright, warm dawning comes—can any man tell what it is or why it is that birds are wild with ecstatic song, and sit singing with perpetual warbling? Can any man tell why it is that they fly singing, turn and wheel in the air with every fantastic gyration, or briskly leap from bough to bough, and twig to twig, or sportively whirl in a feathery fury of mingled delight, a hundred voices crossing and mingling, with strange melody of dissonance? And can any man, then, give a square and solid reason for those experiences that sometimes come to all — and that come often to some, when thoughts are high and imaginations divinely radiant, and the affections full of vibrations of joy, and the whole soul is full of rising gladness, gratitude, happiness, and, at times, ecstasies? Have you never felt this? I am sorry for the man that has not! One day, one hour, of such peaceful joy, were worth a year of common pleasure!

But the soul does not always live willingly with itself. There is a privilege of sympathy with God which shall bring us hours of most serene delight. It is the privilege of God's people to come into such spiritual relationship with Him that they shall have meditations, almost visions, of the Divine goodness and glory, which will take away from them all thought of self-worth or demerit, of joy or sorrow, of thrift or adversity; and will fill them with overpowering gladness for the greatness and the glory of God! As one who stands before some magnificence of nature, or in the presence of some stupendous marvel, or before an outspread and glorious work of art, or in a cathedral full of dreamy beauty, or within a gallery of paintings, where there is a perfect wilderness of colours and forms, as if there were as many as there are flowers in the wilderness; — as persons amid such surroundings are utterly unconscious of self, and forgetful whether they are in the body or out of it, whether rich or poor, whether in trouble or in joy, but are carried quite out of themselves, and made to dwell in the realm and glory of the scene before them; so, and much more, is it in the power of God to open such views of Himself to the soul, as to fill and overflow its capacity, and to make its life, for the time, a life beyond the body— a life that goes forth, as it were, out of doors, and mounts up to the very heavens, and stands before the eternal glory of Love, and among the radiant multitudes in the endless processions of heavenly hosts that are for ever praising God!

Who shall lay tax upon the tongue or upon the thoughts in such glorious visions as these? Who shall criticise or regulate the prayer that springs from such experiences as these? Let a man arrogantly teach rain how to fall, or clouds how to shape themselves, and with what paces to march their airy rounds, or the season how to plant, and tend, and garner; but let him not teach a soul how to pray, upon whom the Holy Ghost thus broods and breathes!

They to whom is given such communion cannot but bear the burden of the Lord in earthly things. Christ's cause and glory in the salvation of souls will oftentimes move their prayers with deep and inexhaustible desires. They may not seek such experiences. They do not come by common asking. They are given to them who are one with Christ; who have entered into such sympathy with God, that they must needs bear His cross and, as it were, be crucified for sinners.

And, in like manner, God makes His servants to bear the burden of God's cause on earth at large; so that, at times, the desires, the yearnings and prayers for the prosperity of Zion will be almost more than flesh can bear; so that, in the expressive language of Scripture, they *travail in birth* for God's work on earth!

There are yet other modes of prayer; but who shall frame words to express what that communion is which the soul holds when, in the fulness of its own feeling, it overflows with praises? It is apparent how great is the folly of those who decry prayer as being useless, inasmuch as God knows what we need —as if asking for enjoyable things is all that a soul does in prayer. What if a man should have an idea as ignoble as this of sounds and space, and should say that no words or sounds are sensible, or of any value and desirableness, except such as articulate well-defined wants; as if they were of no use in exclamations of gladness, in tones and words of joy, in the mazes and tropical exuberance of love, in the sweet endearments of friendship; as if they were of no use in music, in shouts of gladness, and, in short, in any utterance except those for servile uses!

With regard to forms of prayer, these may be of use, and are proper to be used by all who need them; but they can never include the whole of that utterance which the soul *should* express to God in prayer.

Some persons are often troubled respecting familiarity and irreverence in prayer. But it should be remembered by such that the confidence of love is not irreverence. God permits His people to plead with Him, and to pour out their confidence freely. The exhortation is explicit, "Let us come *boldly* to the throne of grace."

Some are discouraged when, after continued communion with God, they do not find any such range and progression in prayer. To pray is, to many, like speaking a new and foreign language. It must be learned. One is not surprised that a foreign tongue is slowly and brokenly spoken at first. Prayer gains in scope and richness as the elements of spirituality increase and the habit of expression is formed.

The Aid of the Spirit.

ROMANS viii. 26.
"Likewise the Spirit also helpeth our infirmities: for we know not what we should pray for as we ought: but the Spirit itself maketh intercession for us with groanings which cannot be uttered."

ROMANS viii. 15.
"For ye have not received the spirit of bondage again to fear; but ye have received the Spirit of adoption, whereby we cry, Abba, Father."

"The prayers I make will then be sweet indeed,
If Thou the Spirit give by which I pray;
My unassisted heart is barren clay,
That of its native self can nothing feed;
Of good and pious works Thou art the seed,
That quickens only where Thou say'st it may.
Unless Thou shew to us Thy own true way,
No man can find it. Father! Thou must lead.
Do Thou, then, breathe those thoughts into my mind
By which such virtue may in me be bred,
That in Thy holy footsteps I may tread;
The fetters of my tongue do Thou unbind,
That I may have the power to sing to Thee!
And sound thy praises everlastingly."

WORDSWORTH.

The Aid of the Spirit.

EVEN a glance of the sun is cheering, in a day of storms, or of clouds, which, without storming, fill the air with sullenness, and make twilight even at noon-day. But what is this compared with the brightness of the unobstructed sun all the day long, filling the air above, overlaying the earth, and pouring gold upon every tree, stone, or house, until the eye shrinks for very brightness!

But the sunlight of a single day brings forth nothing. Such days come in December, in January, and amid the boisterous weeks of February and the tumult of March. But nothing springs up. The tree makes no growth. The light does not enter in. It lies wide abroad, indeed most beautiful, but nothing is created by it; for burnished icicles and frost-drops are the only stems and flowers which come from the slant and cold brightness of the winter's sun.

It is only when, at length, the sun returns from its equatorial pilgrimage, and enters into the earth, and abides within it, that life is awakened. The earth knows his coming. In winter, nature lies as if dead. The sun stretches itself upon it, as did the prophet upon the woman's son, and from every part there is resurrection of root, stem, bud, and flower. But none of these things happen to casual and infrequent shining. They are the fruit of indwelling heat. Not till the sun enters in, and abides in the soil, not till days and nights are struck through with warmth, is there life and glory.

If this be so of the lower physical nature, how much more eminently it is true of the human soul, and of its Sun of Righteousness! It is a gladsome thing in toil and trouble to have a single bright flash from the face of God. A prisoner in a dungeon may have but one small window, and that far up, and out of the way of the sun, while for months and months not one single day does the yellow sun send one single and solitary ray through the poor little window. But at length, in changing its place in the heavens, there comes a day in which, to his surprise and joy, a flash of light springs through and quivers on the wall. It vibrates upon his heart still more tremulously than on the wall. Even thus much gives joy. It warms nothing, and lights but little; but it brings back summer to his soul. It tells him that the sun is not dead, but walks the heavens yet. That single ray speaks of fields, of trees, of birds, and of the whole blue heavens! So is it often in life. It is in the power of one blessed thought, in a truly Christian heart, to send light and joy for hours and days. But that is not enough. It is not enough for Christian growth, or

Christian nourishment, that despondency sometimes hopes and darkness sometimes smiles into light. A Christian is to be a child of light, and to *dwell* in the light. The whiteness of heavenly robes is the light which they reflect from the face of God. A Christian is to bear *much* fruit. This he cannot unless he abides in summer. For mere relief, even a casual visit of God's grace is potential. But for fruit—much fruit, and ripened fruit— nothing will suffice but the whole summer sun.

Now, this indwelling of the Holy Spirit is both to be prayed for and to be possessed. There is provision in the gospel for this very blessing. It is the promise of the Father, and the pledge of the Son. It is made to be a Christian's duty to pray for it and to expect it. For, in very deed, there can be no true and full Christian ripeness without it. The soul forms no habits, and comes to no spiritual conformity to God, by jets and flashes of excitement. These have their use, and are to be gladly accepted. But the soul must lie long in the light; it must abide in Divine warmth. There must be spiritual summer where there is to be much fruit. Our thoughts are like our bodies; men cannot come to good breeding by an occasional entrance into good society. It is habitual commerce with grace and amenity that fashions a man to politeness. It is living in studious habits that makes a man learned. And even more, it is abiding in God, and having the indwelling of His Spirit with us, that bring the soul to good manners, if we may so speak, in Divine things.

It seems an impossible thing to many to carry the presence and influence of the Spirit of God through all the whirl and occupation of life. Is it impossible for a young soldier to carry the spirit of love with him through camp, march, and battle? Is it difficult for the parent to carry his soul full of domestic affections through the business of the day? Is it impossible, or even difficult, for us to carry within us any feeling which is deep and strong, and which we love, in spite of exterior disturbance?

Nay, do we not see every day that the heart, by such enthusiasms or deep emotions, not only goes unchanged through burdensome life, but casts out of itself a flood of radiance, and makes its path light by its own cheerfulness or joy? Love in the soul is like perfume in the garments. Heat cannot melt it, nor cold freeze it, nor the winds blow it away. Going forth or coming home, it scatters itself, but is not wasted; it is for ever going, but never gone. And the love of God shed abroad in the soul surpasses all fragrance in inexhaustible diffusiveness. If men have only a little love, an occasional spark, it may be troublesome to nourish it when the world casts down on it green fuel. A large fire waxes larger by that very wind which blows out a small flame. It is even as St. Peter saith: "If these things be in you, *and abound*, they make you that ye shall neither be barren nor unfruitful in the knowledge of our Lord Jesus Christ."

The work of the Spirit is not to supersede, but to help our faculties. It is akin to parental training, to education, to the action and influence of one mind upon another. Not that God's mind acts upon ours just as ours acts upon others; for we have no warrant for saying this. But the illustration is sufficient to shew that one mind may stimulate another to action without destroying its liberty. The young artist, while he sits under Raphael, or Michael Angelo, or Correggio, does not expect to have his work done by his master. He goes to witness and to catch his master's enthusiasm, that his own eye may be fired and his own hand guided. We bring up our children by the action of our minds upon theirs. Our influence over the child does not take away anything from the child's power, but, on the contrary, adds to it. And so, God says to us, "Work out your own salvation, for I am working in you." It is like a father saying to his children, "Here am I working among you, adding my experience, my wisdom, and my power to yours; therefore be hopeful and courageous, and enter with zeal upon your work." It is an argument of hope and ardour, and not of waiting and faltering. It is *an argument to begin now, and not to delay*, with the vain thought that God will finally do all the work and leave us nothing to do.

If it be asked how shall we distinguish Divine influence from natural, the reply is, We cannot always do it. There is no intimation in the New Testament that anybody can tell. If a husbandman wishes to know whether he is under the influence of right farming, he must go and look at his harvests. If, therefore, a man says, "How can I tell whether this feeling is of God or of Satan?" he cannot tell by the feeling, but by its results.

The human faculties, whether acted upon by sinister spirits, by Divine influences, or by natural causes, always act within the lines and limits of their own laws and nature. And it is not any difference in sensation or consciousness which can distinguish Divine influence from any other. We must abide by Christ's rule of estimate, "By their fruit shall ye know them." Is the fruit good? is there enough of it? is it continuous? It is very certain that a disposition of deep benevolence, a heart of unfeigned love, will lead a man in the right direction, and he need not spend one anxious thought lest the devil should have inspired him with such influence.

On the other hand, conceited and presumptuous men are found, who, assuming that they are under the Divine influence and guidance, follow out their own selfish and fleshly lusts, and attribute it all to God. But no man can have any evidence that he is moved by the Spirit of God, except in so far as the fruit is divine. It does not lie merely in consciousness, in sensation, in any witness or inward light, in any degree or kind of exhilaration, or in the pleasureableness or other quality of the feeling. The moral quality of the life determines whether one is a child of God or of the devil.

What, then, is the use of the truth of God's Spirit, if you cannot discern its presence or action? It is good for general hopefulness. It gives to men courage to know that they are divinely helped, though they may not perceive the special acts. It is an exorcism to fear and superstition; for it exhibits the world as illumined and overcome by the gracious presence of God working both in providence and in grace, and throwing around all who will do well an atmosphere of protection and genial excitement, in which they shall thrive and bring forth abundant fruit.

"Come, Holy Ghost, our souls inspire,
 And lighten with celestial fire,
 Thou the anointing Spirit art,
 Who dost thy seven-fold gifts impart.

"Thy blessed unction from above,
 Is comfort, life, and fire of love.
 Enable with perpetual light
 The dulness of our blinded sight.

"Anoint and cheer our soiled face
 With the abundance of Thy grace.
 Keep far our foes, give peace at home;
 Where Thou art guide, no ill can come.

"Teach us to know the Father, Son,
 And Thee, of both, to be but One;
 That, through the ages all along,
 This may be our endless song:

 "Praise to Thy eternal merit,
  Father, Son, and Holy Spirit."

Humility before God.

JOEL ii. 12, 13.

"Therefore also now, saith the Lord, Turn ye even to me with all your heart, and with fasting, and with weeping, and with mourning: and rend your heart, and not your garments, and turn unto the Lord your God: for he is gracious and merciful, slow to anger, and of great kindness."

MICAH vi. 8.

"He hath shewed thee, O man, what is good; and what doth the Lord require of thee, but to do justly, and to love mercy, and to walk humbly with thy God?"

1 John i. 8, 9.

"If we say that we have no sin, we deceive ourselves, and the truth is not in us. If we confess our sins, he is faithful and just to forgive us our sins, and to cleanse us from all unrighteousness."

PSALM cii. 17.

"He will regard the prayer of the destitute, and not despise their prayer."

"Come, let us to the Lord our God
    With contrite hearts return;
Our God is gracious, nor will leave
    The desolate to mourn.

"His voice commands the tempest forth
    And stills the stormy wave;
And though His arm be strong to smite,
    'Tis also strong to save.

"Long hath the night of sorrow reign'd;
    The dawn shall bring us light;
God shall appear, and we shall rise
    With gladness in His sight.

"Our hearts, if God we seek to know,
    Shall know Him, and rejoice;
His coming like the morn shall be,
    Like morning songs His voice.

"As dew upon the tender herb,
    Diffusing fragrance round;
As show'rs that usher in the spring,
    And cheer the thirsty ground:

"So shall His presence bless our souls,
    And shed a joyful light;
That hallow'd morn shall chase away
    The sorrows of the night."

Humility before God.

I THINK that a view of what we are before God, of our leanness, of our littleness, of our weakness and imperfection, is enough to keep down the risings of any man's pride. There are times when, if a man should receive a full, clear view of what he is himself, in comparison with what God is, all hope and almost life itself would be crushed out of him! And it is only when God reveals Himself in the person of Jesus Christ, pardoning sins, and overlooking our errors and imperfections, that we are enabled to have hope! But while, in the view of God, every Christian feels that he is not only sinful, but ignominiously so, and degraded beyond all expression, yet there is in his experience of the love which Christ has for him, notwithstanding his weakness and impurity, a certain boldness that lifts him up and gives him confidence to stand in the very presence of God!

Did you ever see a child, which through a period of days and weeks had little by little been gathering mischief and disobedience, and seeming to be working for a whipping? By and by he comes to a state in which it is plain that there must be an outbreak; and an occasion occurs, perhaps, from some trifling circumstances, in which he is brought to a direct issue with the parent, and the question is, Who shall conquer, the mother or the child? She expostulates, but the child grows red and swells with anger; she pleads with him, and uses all her power to bring him to a reconciliation on the basis of justice; but nothing will do; and at last, when everything else has failed, and she has been unable by gentle means to subdue his haughty pride—if she does what she ought to do, she gives him a sound whipping! He is quickly subdued, and filled with shame, yet not entirely humbled; but when he sees the much-loving mother, who has wept with even more pain and suffering than the child himself, going about the room — a kind of living music to the child's unconscious feeling! —taking her seat at last in some window-nook, with sorrow upon her face, he comes to himself, and, thinking a moment, feels that all the old dark flood of ugliness has gone away, and an entirely new feeling begins to take possession of him. He looks at the face of the mother, with love swelling in his heart, and wishes that he were sitting at her feet. And when she says, "My child, why do you not come to me?"—with another burst of tears, not of pain and wounded feeling, but of joy and love, he throws himself into her arms, and buries his head in her bosom! Ah! if I remember aright, I can recount many similar experiences in my own early life; and I am brought back into the remembrance of such childhood's scenes, because the relation of my own disobedient heart to my mother when she punished me, is the best illustration which I can give you of the relation of the soul of a rebelling child of God to His chastising hand! When, after being puffed up with pride and vanity, from being engaged in worldly pursuits, and being contented with mere worldly moralities, I am suddenly, by afflictions, or disappointments, or by the direct visitation of God's Holy Spirit, humbled and brought to the very earth with contrition; oh, who can tell how sweet it is to take hold of the outreaching hand of the Lord Jesus Christ, and go up into the confidence and embrace of His love! I am nothing myself: I am entirely humbled and subdued; only I feel His love in my heart, and my heart swells with love in return.

These are days of sweetness! These are days of heavenly joy! These are days of true humility! Oh, how lowly a man bows, and how lowly he walks, who has a view of his own littleness and emptiness in comparison with the greatness and the fulness of the ever-living and ever-loving God!

The Prayer-Meeting.

MALACHI iii. 16, 17.

"Then they that feared the Lord spake often one to another: and the Lord hearkened, and heard it, and a book of remembrance was written before him for them that feared the Lord, and that thought upon his name. And they shall be mine, saith the Lord of hosts, in that day when I make up my jewels; and I will spare them, as a man spareth his own son that serveth him."

ECCLESIASTES v. 2.

"Be not rash with thy mouth, and let not thine heart be hasty to utter any thing before God: for God is in heaven, and thou upon earth: therefore let thy words be few."

1 JOHN ii. 28, 29.

"And now, little children, abide in him; that when he shall appear, we may have confidence, and not be ashamed before him at his coming. If ye know that he is righteous, ye know that every one that doeth righteousness is born of him."

MATTHEW xviii. 19, 20.

"Again I say unto you, That if two of you shall agree on earth as touching anything that they shall ask, it shall be done for them of my Father which is in heaven. For where two or three are gathered together in my name, there am I in the midst of them."

" Jesus, where'er Thy people meet,
  There they behold Thy mercy-seat;
  Where'er they seek Thee, Thou art found,
  And every place is hallow'd ground.

" For Thou, within no walls confined,
  Inhabitest the humble mind;
  Such ever bring Thee where they come,
  And going, take Thee to their home.

" Dear Shepherd of Thy chosen few,
  Thy former mercies here renew;
  Here to our waiting hearts proclaim
  The sweetness of Thy saving name.

" Here may we prove the power of prayer
  To strengthen faith, and sweeten care;
  To teach our faint desires to rise,
  And bring all heaven before our eyes.

" Behold, at Thy commanding word,
  We stretch the curtain and the cord;
  Come Thou and fill this wider space,
  And bless us with a large increase.

" Lord, we are few, but Thou art near;
  Nor short Thine arm, nor deaf Thine ear:
  Oh rend the heavens, come quickly down,
  And make a thousand hearts Thine own!"

COWPER.

The Prayer-Meeting.

A PRAYER-MEETING is a place for social religious life. It is not for preaching, nor is it necessarily for exhortation. It is a place WHERE CHRISTIANS MEET to instruct and strengthen one another by a free and familiar development of their religious experiences and emotions. It is an altar for whose fire every Christian brings a brand, and where the whole pile is made up of the added faggots of many enkindled hearts.

This is the primary idea of a prayer-meeting. It is evident, therefore, that the first step towards a wholesome meeting is truthfulness. Yet it is this important element which is apt to be most often lacking. It is thought necessary, even by advanced Christians, to assume a sense of awful responsibility, to put on an air of profound solemnity, and to manifest an eminently devout spirit. But these feelings are never proper, except when they are real. They should never be assumed. They should never be put on and worn as a kind of appropriate dress, becoming to the occasion. Men should not lay aside their naturalness before God, any more than before men — and even less, as God can see through the guise when men may not. They should not pretend to be what they are not, any more in a prayer-meeting with their brethren than alone in their own private closet. Any pretentious mood, or any forced and artificial feeling, will always do harm, for it will overlay the mind, as straw and dry leaves overlay the soil, so that nothing is able to spring up.

No man should utter a word in a prayer-meeting which is not spoken in sincerity. It is a great and grievous sin for a man to utter prayers to God when his heart neither suggests nor enters into the petitions. It is a piece of mockery that no man would endure, much less God. For any creature to bow before his Creator, and say prayers, whether they be long or short, printed or unprinted, which do not engage his heart, but which he utters from a mere sense of duty, or from superstitious fear, or from habit, is an inexpressible audacity. Yet it is often done. And it is said, "If you do not feel like praying, pray till you do." Now, there certainly are degrees of interest; and a man may be blameless for experiencing less fervour at the beginning of a devotional period than at the end of it. But for a man to employ prayer as a mere exercise, or as a mere mode of giving himself a stirring up—to stand before God and assume the tones, the language, the manner of feeling, for the sake of coming by and by into the feeling, is a desecration of prayer almost blasphemous.

If it be asked, "What, then, shall a

man do? Shall he neglect prayer until he does feel? Shall he refuse to take part in a prayer-meeting until the glow is upon him?" the answer is, that such a man should not neglect prayer, neither in his closet, nor perhaps in the prayer-meeting. But he must prepare himself for prayer. He must watch and study for the disposition. He should refresh his mind with scriptural truths, and should consider his own wants and sinfulness. This he should do apart from noise and excitement, if possible; and he may be aided in doing it by employing hymns and psalms, which will oftentimes speedily carry his mind out of a dull and dead frame into some beginnings of life. He may thus come into a state in which prayer will not be a stupid act, or a dead form, but the glowing expression of a living feeling.

This is a proper preparation for prayer, whether public or private. If prayers in a prayer-meeting cannot be genuine, they might better be omitted, and hymns sung in their place. If but a single sentence is uttered, let it be real; and let utterance cease when the heart no longer prompts— and the heart will often have ceased its promptings long before a recitation of fifteen minutes is concluded. One moment of real communion with God is prayer, but a whole hour of recited words, without feeling, is not prayer, and is worse than none.

The way to kill a prayer-meeting is to make it conventional: and the chief secret of conducting it so that it shall minister to edification, is to force people out of conventional ways; to break up hereditary and stereotyped unwritten forms of prayer; to charm men into forgetfulness of the machinery of the meeting; so that they shall pray artlessly, naturally, and sensibly.

But, above all, let all pretence, all mock solemnity and devotion, be put away. Let no man suffer himself to appear to his brethren to be what he is not; for this is part of the injunction, "Let every man speak truth with his neighbour." If this rule be not observed, and the frequent tendencies to violate it be not corrected, the prayer-meeting will degenerate, and people will lose first all profit and then all interest in them. For, what if people should go to an evening party, not in their natural character, but one striving to be brilliant, another to be witty, another to be instructive, another to be profound? Who could endure the sham? There is need in prayer-meetings of men who are willing to stand simply and only on what they are and what they have.

The speaking in prayer-meetings should be conversational, and so, natural. The words spoken should flow naturally from the heart's experience, or else it were better to be silent. Usually, however, when a man has nothing to say, he gets up and exhorts sinners to repent; or auother, whose heart is empty, informs the church that they are very cold, and live far beneath their privileges. Such prayers or exhortations may be very glib and fluent, but they are as dry of sap or juice as last year's corn-husks. They are not only profitless but damaging. On the contrary, there are oftentimes prayers, humble, timid, half-inaudible, the utterances of uncultivated lips, that may cut a poor figure as literature, that are nevertheless not to be scornfully disdained. If a child may not talk at all till he can speak fluent English, he will never learn. There should be a process going on continually of education, by which all the members of the church should be able to contribute of their experiences and gifts; and, in such a course of development, the first hesitating, stumbling, ungrammatical prayer of a confused Christian may be worth more to the church than the best prayer of the most eloquent pastor. The prayer may be but little;

but it is not a little thing that a church has one more man who is beginning to pray than it had before.

The conductor of a prayer-meeting should have a distinct conception of what such a meeting is to be and to do; and as it is a mutual-instruction class, a place for religious feeling to take the social element, his chief duty should be to draw out the timid, to check the obtrusive, to encourage simple and true speaking, and to apply religious truths to those wants and struggles and experiences which are freely mentioned there.*

* See Appendix.

" Jesus! thy saints assemble here
Thy power and goodness to declare:
Oh, may these happy reasons prove
That we have known redeeming love!

" And while of mercies past we speak,
And sing of endless joys to come,
Let Thy full glories on us break,
And every thought give Jesus room.

" Engrave Thy name on every heart,
And give us all, before we part,
The life-restoring joys to know
Which from Thy veins in rivers flow.

" No other food can we desire,
No other theme our bosoms fire,
But sovereign, rich, redeeming love
While here, and when we dwell above!

" Thine everlasting love we sing,
The source whence all our pleasures spring;
How deep it sinks, how high its flow,
No saint can tell, no angel know!

" Its length and breadth no eye can trace,
No thought explain the bounds of grace,
Like its dear Author's name, it shines
In infinite unfolded lines!

" The love which saves our souls from hell,
On this side heaven we ne'er can tell;
But when we reach bright Canaan's plains,
We'll sound it in immortal strains."

SWAINE.

The Prayerless Life.

HEBREWS iii. 12-15.

"Take heed, brethren, lest there be in any of you an evil heart of unbelief, in departing from the living God. But exhort one another daily, while it is called To-day; lest any of you be hardened through the deceitfulness of sin. For we are made partakers of Christ, if we hold the beginning of our confidence stedfast unto the end; while it is said, To-day if ye will hear his voice, harden not your hearts, as in the provocation."

"In streets, and op'nings of the gates,
   Where pours the busy crowd,
Thus heav'nly Wisdom lifts her voice,
   And cries to men aloud:
How long, ye scorners of the truth,
   Scornful will ye remain?
How long shall fools their folly love,
   And hear my words in vain?

"O turn, at last, at my reproof!
   And, in that happy hour,
His bless'd effusions on your heart
   My Spirit down shall pour,
But since so long, with earnest voice,
   To you in vain I call,
Since all my counsels and reproofs
   Thus ineffectual fall;

"The time will come, when humbled low,
   In Sorrow's evil day,
Your voice by anguish shall be taught,
   But taught too late, to pray.
When, like the whirlwind, o'er the deep
   Comes Desolation's blast:
Pray'rs then extorted shall be vain,
   The hour of mercy past.

"The choice you made has fix'd your doom;
   For this is Heav'n's decree,
That with the fruits of what he sow'd
   The sinner fill'd shall be."

The Prayerless Life.

WE have known men—upon whose grounds waved magnificent trees of centuries' growth, lifted up into the air with vast breadth, and full of twilight at mid-day—who cut down all these mighty monarchs, and cleared the ground bare; and then, when the desolation was complete, and the fierce summer gazed full into their face with its fire, they bethought themselves of shade, and forthwith set out a generation of thin, shadowless sticks, pining and waiting till they should stretch out their boughs with protection, and darken the ground with grateful shadow. Such folly is theirs who refuse the tree of life, the shadow of the Almighty, and sit, instead, under the feeble trees of their own planting, whose tops will never be broad enough to shield them, and whose boughs will never voice to them the music of the air. Some of the most remarkable figures of the Bible are made to illustrate this sad truth.

The mountains lift their tops so high in the air that towering clouds, which have no rest in the sky, love to come to them, and, wrapping about their tops, distil their moisture upon them. Thus mountains hold commerce with God's upper ocean, and, like good men, draw supplies from the invisible. And so it is that, in the times of drought in the vales below, the rocks are always wet. The mountain moss is always green. The seams and crevices are always dripping, and rock-veins are throbbing a full pulse, while all the scene down below faints for want of moisture. In some hidden gorge, unvisited by the sun, these cold rills bubble up and issue forth upon their errand. Could one who builds his house upon the plain but meet and tap these springs in the mountain, and lay his artificial channels to the very source, he would never know when drought cometh. For mountain springs never grow dry so long as clouds brood the hill tops. Day and night they gush and fall with liquid plash and unheard music; except when thirsty birds — to whose song the rivulet all day long has been a bass — stoop to drink at their crystal edges! And he who has put himself into communication with these mountain springs shall never be unsupplied. While artificial cisterns dry up, and crack for dryness, this mountain fountain comes night and day with cool abundance. While others, with weary strokes, force up from deep wells a penurious supply of turbid water, he that has joined himself to a mountain spring has its voice in his dwelling night and day, summer and winter, without work or stroke of labouring pump, clear, sweet, and cheerful;

running of its own accord to serve, and singing at its work, more musical than any lute; and in its song bringing suggestions of its mountain home.

With such a spring—near, accessible, urging itself upon the eye and ear—how great would be his folly who should abandon it, and fill his attic with a leaden cistern, that forever leaked when full, and was dry when it did not leak! Listen, then, to the Word of God—"My people have committed two evils: they have forsaken me, the fountain of living waters, and have hewed them out cisterns, broken cisterns, that can hold no water."

Man is not made to be independent in his powers. With all his endowments he is made to lean on every side for support; and should his connexions on either side be cut, he would droop and wither like a tree whose roots had been sundered.

The eye carries no light with it, but receives its sight from the luminous element without. The ear hath no sound within it, but only receives it from without. The tongue and throat beat upon the air for vibrations, as a musician strikes for musical sounds; and if hindered in their connexions or broken from their dependencies, ear, tongue, and eye would fall back into voiceless darkness. And every bodily function is directly or immediately joined to the physical world in such a way, that, while man is lord of creation, he is also its subject and dependent, and must ask leave to exist from the earth, the air, the sun, and the clouds.

These dependent relations symbolise the yet more important relations which the soul sustains to God. Man is not made to exist in rounded, perfect, and independent spiritual life in his own right and nature. He only is a perfect man who has himself in the keeping of God. The soul only, when divinely influenced, receives its power. Our faculties, like the eye that must be filled with light from without, wait for their power from above. It is the Divine energy, acting through the human faculty, that gives to man his real existence. Nor does any man know his power, his nature, his richness of emotion, the height and depth of his being, until he unfolds under the influence of the Spirit of the living God.

What is this influence which acts within or upon the soul? I will tell you when you will tell me what it is in light and heat that works upon the root to bring forth the stem; what it is that works within the stem to bring forth the bud; what it is that works upon the bud to persuade it into blossom; and what that mysterious spirit is, that, dismissing the beauty of the bloom, holds back its life in the new form of fruit. It is light, it is heat, it is moisture, it is the soil, it is the plant, it is the vital energy of nature. Thus we stand throwing words at a marvellous change, whose interior nature we cannot search nor find out. "So is every one that is born of the Spirit."

But of the fact itself, it is full of blessedness to know that the soul has a relationship to God—personal, direct, vital—and that it grows and blossoms by it, while it languishes and dwarfs without it.

The body grows by its true connexions with material nature; the social affections grow by their true relations to men and society; and the spiritual powers must grow by their true relations to God. In the material world, the roots of trees are in the ground, while the top moves freely above. But the soul roots upward, and so, like long pendulous vines of air-plants, that root upon tropical branches, has its liberty down toward the earth. We are the branches of Christ. "As the branch cannot bear fruit of itself, except it abide in the vine, no more can ye except ye abide in me."

But is not this a bondage and restriction? To selfishness it may be; but not to love. Selfishness grows strong by shrinking, for concentration is the nature of selfishness. But love grows by pressing outward and evolving.

That we are bound to God is as great a restriction of our liberty, as it is to a plant's freedom to be held by the sun; to the child's liberty, that the double-orbed love of father and mother bear it up from cradled nothingness to manly power; or to the human heart's liberty, when, finding another life, two souls move through the sphere of love, flying now with double wings, but one spirit.

No man has come to himself who has not known what it is to be utterly forgetful of self in loving. As a bird born in a cage, and singing there, amid short, impatient hops, from perch to wire, from wire to ring, and from ring to perch again, so is man unrenewed. As this bird, when darting through the opened door, feels with wondrous thrill the wide sweep of the open air, and dare not sing for joy, but goes from ground to limb, from lower limb to higher, until the topmost bough be reached, and then stooping for a moment, springs upward and flies with wild delight, and fills the air as it goes with all its sounds of ransomed joy—so is the soul that first learns its liberty in God, and goes singing heavenward in all "the light and liberty of the sons of God."

He who forsakes God for a greater liberty, is like a babe lost from its mother. They who refrain from God for the sake of pleasure, are like men running from the free air to seek sunlight amid shadows and in dungeons. They who withdraw from God that they may have wider circuits of personal power, are like birds that forsake the forests and fly within the fowler's cage, to find a larger bound and wider liberty.

Appendix.

"It has long appeared to my mind a great evil that a certain *cant phraseology*, or *stock of phrases*, has come somehow to be handed about from parish to parish, yea, down from generation to generation, until our good people have learned to regard it as all from the Bible — not only adopting it into their family and social prayers, but *fathering* it upon God's Word. Here, however, detail is everything; and I will venture to give some examples of the phraseology referred to, arranging it, for the sake of distinctness, under two or three heads.

"There is what might be called an unhappy, sometimes quite grotesque, mingling of Scripture texts. Who is not familiar with the following words addressed to God in prayer,—'Thou art the high and lofty One that inhabiteth eternity *and the praises thereof*'—which is but a jumble of two glorious texts, each glorious taken by itself, both marred, and one altogether lost indeed, when thus combined and mingled. The one is Isaiah lvii. 15, 'Thus saith the high and lofty One *that inhabiteth eternity*, whose name is Holy.' The other is Psalm xxii. 3, 'Thou art holy, O thou that *inhabitest the praises of Israel.*' The inhabiting of the praises *of eternity*, to say the least, is meagre; there were no praises in the *past* eternity to inhabit. But what a glory is there in God's condescending to inhabit, take up His very abode, in the praises of Israel, of the ransomed Church! Then there is an example nothing less than grotesque, under this head, and yet one in such frequent use, that I suspect it is very generally regarded as having the sanction of Scripture. Here it is —'We would put our hand on our mouth, and our mouth in the dust, and cry out, Unclean, unclean! God be merciful to me, a sinner!' This is no fewer than *four* texts joined, each beautiful by itself. First, Job xl. 4, 'Behold, I am vile; what shall I answer thee? I will lay my hand upon my mouth.' Second, Lamentations iii. 29, 'He putteth his mouth in the dust; if so be there may be hope.' Third, Leviticus xiii. 45, where the leper is directed to put a covering upon his upper lip, and to cry, 'Unclean, unclean!' And fourth, the publican's prayer. But how incongruous a man's first putting his hand on his mouth then putting his mouth in the dust, and, last of all, crying out, &c.!

"The only other example I give under this head, is an expression nearly universal among us, and, I suspect, almost universally thought to be in Scripture— 'In thy favour is life, and thy lovingkindness is better than life.' The fact is, that this also is just an unhappy combination of two passages, in which the term *life* is used in altogether different, and even incompatible, senses—namely Psalm xxx. 5, 'In his favour is life,' life, of course, in the higher sense of true blessedness; and Psalm lxiii. 3, 'Thy lovingkindness is better than life,'— where, evidently, life means the present temporal life.

"A second class may be described as unhappy alterations of Scripture language. Need I say that the 130th Psalm, 'Out of the depths,' &c., is one of the most precious in the whole book of the Psalms? Why must we have the words of David and the Holy Ghost thus given in public prayer, and so constantly, that our pious people come all to adopt it into their social and family prayers, 'There is forgiveness with thee, that thou mayest be feared, and plenteous redemption, *that thou mayest be sought after, or unto?*' How precious the simple words as they stand in the Psalm, (ver. 4,)

There is forgiveness with thee, that thou mayest be feared:' (ver. 7, 8,) 'With the Lord there is mercy, and with him is plenteous redemption; and he shall redeem Israel from all his iniquities!' Again in this blessed Psalm, the words of the third verse, 'If thou, Lord, should mark iniquities, O Lord, who shall stand?' too seldom are left us in their naked simplicity, but must undergo the following change, 'If thou wert *strict* to mark iniquity,' &c. I remember in my old College days, we used to have it in a much more offensive shape, 'If thou wert strict to mark and *rigorous to punish!*'

"Another favourite change is the following,—'Thou art in heaven, and we upon the earth; therefore let our words be few *and well ordered.*' Solomon's simple and sublime utterance (full of instruction, surely on the whole theme I am dealing with) is, 'God is in heaven, and thou upon earth; therefore let thy words *be few,*' (Eccles. v. 2.) For another example under this class, see how Habakkuk's sublime words are tortured, 'Thou art of purer eyes than to behold evil, and canst not look on sin *without abhorrence.*' The words of the Holy Ghost are (Hab. i. 13,) 'Thou art of purer eyes than to behold evil, and canst not look on iniquity.' Need I say that the power of the figure, 'canst not look on iniquity,' is nearly lost, when you add that God *can* look on it, only not without abhorrence?

"A third class is made up of meaningless pleonasms, vulgar common-place redundancies of expression, in quoting from the Scriptures. One of these has become so universal, that I venture to say you seldom miss it, when the passage referred to comes up at all. 'Be in the midst of us,' (or, as some prefer to express it, I humbly think not in the best taste, 'in our midst') 'to bless us, *and to do us good.*' What additional idea is there in the last expression, 'and to do us good?' The passage referred to is Exod. xx. 24, 'In all places where I record my name, I will come unto you, and I will bless you.' Such is the simplicity of Scripture. Our addition is, 'bless us and do us good.' In Dan. iv. 35, we read the noble words, 'None can stay his hand, or say unto him, What doest thou?' The favourite change is, 'None can stay thy hand *from working.*' 'Eye hath not seen, nor ear heard, neither have entered into the heart of man the things which God hath prepared for them that love him.' This is changed, 'neither hath it entered into the heart of man *to conceive* the things.' Constantly we hear God addressed as 'the hearer *and answerer* of prayer'—a mere vulgar and useless pleonasm, for the Scripture idea of God's hearing prayer is just His answering it—'O thou that hearest prayer, unto thee shall all flesh come;' 'Hear my prayer, O Lord;' 'I love the Lord because he hath heard my voice and my supplications.' What again, that common-place of public er, 'Thy consolations are neither few nor small.' The reference, I suppose, is to these words of Job, 'Are the consolations of God small with thee?' So one scarce ever hears that prayer of the seventy-fourth Psalm, 'Have respect to the covenant, for the dark places of the earth are full of the habitations of cruelty,' without the addition, '*horrid* cruelty;' nor the call to prayer in Isaiah, 'Keep not silence, and give him no rest, till he establish, and till he make Jerusalem a praise in the earth,' without the addition 'the *whole* earth;' nor that appeal of the Psalmist, 'Whom have I in heaven but thee? and there is none upon earth that I desire beside thee,' without the addition 'none in *all* the earth.' These last may seem small matters, indeed. And so they are, nor were worth finding fault with, did they occur but occasionally. But viewed as stereotyped commonexpressions, weak enough in themselves, and passing so often as to give an impression of their having Scripture authority, I humbly think they ought to be discountenanced and discarded—banished wholly from our Presbyterian worship. It will, perhaps, surprise you to learn that the only Scripture authority for that favourite, and somewhat peculiar expression, about the 'wicked rolling sin as a sweet morsel under their tongue,' is the following words in the book of Job (xx. 12,) 'Though wickedness be sweet in his mouth, though he *hide* it under his tongue.'

"As for some old, almost heathenish, expressions one *used* to hear, I hope they are pretty well out among us—such as, 'Thou art the greatest, and wisest, and best of all beings.' Of course this is not to be endured from a Christian pulpit. Holy Scripture never speaks of God as greatest, wisest, best, but as the 'I am,' 'only wise,' 'only good,' 'who only doeth great wonders,' and so on."—*The Rev. C. F. Brown's Tract on Prayer.*

www.ingramcontent.com/pod-product-compliance
Lightning Source LLC
Chambersburg PA
CBHW020252170426
43202CB00008B/340